CURRENT AFRICAN ISSUES 45

THE AGRARIAN QUESTION IN TANZANIA?
A State of the Art Paper

Sam Maghimbi
Razack B. Lokina
Mathew A. Senga

NORDISKA AFRIKAINSTITUTET, UPPSALA
In coperation with
THE UNIVERSITY OF DAR ES SALAAM
2011

The Mwalimu Nyerere Professorial Chair in Pan-African Studies was established as a university chair at the University of Dar es Salaam in honour of the great nationalist and pan-Africanist leader of Africa and the first president of Tanzania, Mwalimu Julius Kambarage Nyerere. It was inaugurated on April 19, 2008 by the Prime Minister Honourable Mizengo Pinda in the presence of Mama Maria Nyerere. The main objective of the Chair is to reinvigorate intellectual debates on the Campus and stimulate basic research on burning issues facing the country and the continent from a pan-African perspective. The core activities of the Chair include publication of state of the art papers. As part of the latter, the Chair is pleased to publish the first paper The Agrarian Question in Tanzania. It is planned to publish at least one state of the art paper every year.

First published by
Mwalimu Nyerere Professorial Chair in Pan-African Studies
University of Dar es Salaam
P. O. Box 35091
Dar es Salaam
Email: mwalimunyererechair@udsm.ac.tz
Website: http://www.nyererechair.udsm.ac.tz

INDEXING TERMS:
Agrarian policy
Agrarian structure
Peasantry
Agricultural population
Land tenure
State
Agrarian reform
Land reform
Rural development
Economic and social development
Tanzania

Language checking: Peter Colenbrander
ISSN 0280-2171
ISBN 978-91-7106-684-8
© the authors, Mwalimu Nyerere Chair and Nordiska Afrikainstitutet 2011
Grafisk form Elin Olsson, ELBA Grafisk Produktion

CONTENTS

PREFACE

The Mwalimu Nyerere Professorial Chair in Pan-African Studies was inaugurated by the prime minister in April 2008. It is the first of its kind, in more ways than one. First, of course, it is the first chair in honour of Mwalimu Nyerere. Second, it is a university chair directly under the vice-chancellor. Thirdly, strictly speaking, it is neither a teaching chair nor a research chair in the traditional sense. Its mandate is to reinvigorate intellectual debate and discussion at the University of Dar es Salaam in order to revive the great tradition of critical intellectual discourse that distinguished the university in the 1960s and 1970s.

Like many universities in Africa, the University of Dar es Salaam did not escape the market and privatization fundamentalism preached by the World Bank and its associates. The result was the vocationalization and commercialization of university education, on the one hand, and the devalorization of basic research in favour of consultancies and so-called policy-oriented 'research', on the other. Lavishly funded by donors, even the policy-oriented research was/is housed in institutes outside the university. The rise of such parallel institutions predictably undermined the university as a site of knowledge generation, a process that can only take place through basic research on the bigger issues facing society. Handsome grants and allowances offered by such parallel institutes quickly siphoned off researchers, both faculty and students, from the university. There was an additional attraction: the NGO-type research institutes were much less demanding of the theoretical rigour and academic excellence expected of a good university. Moreover, such institutes could not replicate the quality control exercised at universities through peer review and seminar discussions, where drafts are presented and vigorously debated. No wonder then, that whereas the hallmark of a university is the publication of books (some of which may take years of research, reflection and writing) and in refereed journals, NGO-type research institutes churn out glossy reports, pamphlets and policy briefs by the dozen every year.

Thus, the other mandate of the chair is to stimulate *basic research* through the preparation and dissemination of state-of-the-art papers. The intention is that such papers on crucial social issues will raise major questions, which remain unanswered or not adequately answered, thus 'provoking' researchers to take them up in further research. To ensure good quality, the authors of a state-of-the-art paper are selected through an open invitation to interested teams to apply. After a shortlisting of applications, based on the quality of a concept note, by a team consisting of the chair and one other professor, the candidates appear for an interview. The expectation is that the selected team will prepare the paper following the best academic tradition. The interviewing team comments on the first draft of the paper and then a revised version is presented to a workshop of peers. It is expected that the authors will integrate the comments and rectify any weaknesses for final publication. In spite of the rigorous procedure, it is not easy to ensure excellence. That will only come through building, or rather rebuilding, the tradition of intellectual discourse based on a double commitment – commitment to social change for the better, and a commitment to give the best to society.

The team for this paper comprises a senior, professor-level academic, a lecturer and a junior academic at the level of teaching assistant. The rationale for this combination is that the process of preparing the paper would also be a process of 'mentoring' younger members of the faculty.

The chair is pleased to publish the first state-of-the-art paper, *The Agrarian Question in*

Tanzania. We are grateful to the Nordic Africa Institute for their grant, which has covered the preparation and publication of the paper as well as the holding of the workshop. We would also like to thank the participants of the second summer school on the agrarian question organized jointly by the Land Rights Research and Resources Institute (HAKIARDHI) based in Dar es Salaam and the African Institute of Agrarian Studies (AIAS) based in Harare, who agreed to devote the first day of the school to participating in the workshop. And, finally, we are, as always, indebted to our copy editor, Saida Yahya-Othman, for going the extra mile to complete the task in record time.

Issa Shivji
Mwalimu Nyerere University Professor of Pan-African Studies
April 2010

Abstract

There are about four million peasant families in Tanzania whose principal economic activity is small-scale farming and pastoralism. Their farming is on the smallest scale, the average family farm being only two acres in size and quite often not in one continuous block. Land parcelling is extreme and a technical breakthrough or green revolution in farming has not occurred. The principal agricultural equipment is the hand hoe. Since colonial times, those in authority have pursued policies that have reproduced a stolid, almost homogeneous peasantry: easy to control politically, dominate socially and exploit economically. It is argued that the small scale of operation of the peasant economy and the failure of technical and marketing innovations have contributed to widespread absolute poverty among peasant families. The agrarian question in Tanzania is also a national question and the national economy is not likely to take off if the agrarian question is not resolved. Peasants own a lot of land in Tanzania, but accumulation is slow and agrarian classes are not well developed. Given the current land tenure, the agrarian condition is not likely to improve. Many land laws have been enacted, but land parcelling to the smallest plot and insecure tenure are major problems. The hypothesis is advanced that land laws are not enough to bring about agrarian development and that what is needed now is land reform to consolidate peasant farms and arrest the further subdivision of farms. There is still good agricultural land that is not farmed, but the current land tenure of peasants reproduces itself on new farmland. A minimum size of farm is recommended as a measure to stop further parcelling of agricultural land. Differentiation of the peasantry along the lines predicted by Karl Kautsky is occurring very slowly, and the peasantry is more consistent with a Chayanovian description. Slow differentiation means slow accumulation at the farm and state level. State accumulation strategies, such as the creation of parastatal farms and crop authorities, are considered, as are peasant accumulation strategies, such as the formation of cooperatives. Most importantly, the commodification and privatization of land and the forceful expulsion of peasant populations and commodification of labour power are also considered within a political economy framework. Socialist agriculture has failed in Eastern Europe, China and in Tanzania. This makes a study of agrarian themes even more interesting. New theories are needed as some old themes (including the idea of the alliance of peasants and workers) lose historical importance and other themes (like the current upsurge of neoliberalism in African agriculture) gain theoretical and real-life importance. The conclusion is that in order to accelerate agricultural development, land tenure must be institutionalized. This will remove the wasteful use of land and other resources resulting from the current open-access regime, which is arguably to be associated with the tragedy of the commons. Further research on the agrarian question is recommended.

Keywords: agrarian question; land tenure; land reform; peasants; state; accumulation; agrarian classes.

CONCEPTUAL AND THEORETICAL ISSUES

This part covers conceptual and theoretical issues on the agrarian question, including classical and modern debates and discourses. Drawing from different scholars, the discussion seeks to establish that the agrarian question remains unresolved and constitutes a fundamental dimension of the national question.

The Agrarian Question: Conceptual issues

It is not easy to clearly define and conceptualize the agrarian question. In a country like Tanzania, the question is surrounded by a broad spectrum of complex and paradoxical issues. One needs not only a sound knowledge of the necessary economic and social theory in order to examine the agrarian question, but also an accumulation of knowledge on the history of land and other forms of land use in the country under consideration. In order to achieve a detailed analysis and examination of the matter at hand, the dynamics of land tenure systems and the perceptions and responses of land users need also to be considered. Land and its control and use are considered as significant elements of the agrarian question.

For scholars such as Byres (1991) and Bernstein (2004), the agrarian question should be understood in three basic ways: the penetration of capitalist relations into agriculture; the contribution of agriculture to capitalist development as a whole; and the role of agrarian classes of labour in the struggle for democracy and socialism. Along the same lines, Moore (2008) adds a fourth way: the agrarian question as an ecological question whose world historical import is profoundly intertwined with the others, but whose significance (up to now) has been unevenly appreciated. Moore specifies that these four are not discrete moments: none can be explained without situating it within the others.

Close to the agrarian question is the national question. Scholars like Shivji (2009a:75-6) view these two as being inextricably linked in the worldwide process of capital accumulation. Shivji argues that the contradictory relationship between the African periphery and imperialism constitutes the national question, and at the heart of this relationship lies the crisis of over-accumulation that characterizes capitalist imperialism, while the agrarian question consists of the disarticulated accumulation that characterizes peripheral capitalism. He argues that in the immediate post-independence period, these questions were at the forefront of scholarly debates and political thought, but the national and agrarian questions disappeared from mainstream discourse following the neoliberal intervention, which had no way of problematizing the process of accumulation on the global or local level.

Shivji, however, notes that among leftist political economists, the debate simmered on. He cites Moyo and Yeros (2007), who are against what they characterize as the internationalist left. The internationalist left argued that the national question either had been resolved or was no longer relevant and that the agrarian question had been resolved because the peasant was fast disappearing by ceasing to be a pure agriculturalist and by involving himself/herself in multiple occupations.

For these scholars (Moyo, Yeros and Shivji), the national and agrarian questions remain unresolved. They are inseparably linked and inserted in the global process of imperialist accumulation, which is characterized by polarization, producing articulated accumulation at the centre and disarticulated accumulation at the periphery. As already noted, the dynamics of land tenure systems, among other things, form an important component of the agrarian question. While seeking to underscore the agrarian question, this paper delineates how the land question needs to be analysed in the context of the interaction between process and structure, by examining the ways the process of defining land rights unravels within a given social structure. The focus here will be on the role of the state – both colonial and contemporary – in defining land tenure and the alliances it forms with capital, social classes and groups around the land question, and the extent to which it reflects the interest of the landowning classes and their relations with international and national capital and thereby perpetuates the agrarian crisis.

Theoretical Issues
Peasantry and agrarian theories, whether classical or contemporary, can be categorized as 'critical' and 'practical' theories. Critical theories are an attempt to study and understand the world and its inner processes of development, while practical theories involve studying how to change the world, and they entail the relationship of theory to practice. This section extensively covers a wide range of theories on the peasantry and the agrarian question. Detailed examination of these theories will be informed by the validity or invalidity of these theories in explaining the agrarian question. The rationale for doing this derives from the expectation that theories should serve as illuminators of social problems, phenomena or events.

Major Classical and Contemporary Debates and Discourses on the Agrarian Question
Among Marxists, the agrarian question was a central issue in early debates about capitalist development. The essence of the subject at hand was not really economic. What really preoccupied the classical Marxist thinkers was a political question: Would the peasants act as allies in the struggle to achieve socialism, or were they ultimately a reactionary, counter-revolutionary force? (Stalin 1954).

According to Stalin, as far as Marx was concerned, the development of the capitalist mode of production was dependent on the dispossession and proletarianization of the peasantry, something that will be widely covered in the subsequent sections of this paper. Peasants who succeeded in resisting that process and clung to their land through armed resistance, for example, might in fact be impeding the achievement of socialism, however worthy their struggle might be in its own terms. As both Marx and Lenin suggested, peasant producers might also sustain the continued dominance of archaic merchant capitalist forms of rural exploitation, or the dominance of landlord classes. It remains true that Marx did not think that peasant farming could survive in the long term. He argued that it was only compatible with a limited development of industrial capitalism, and insisted that in the longer term the peasantry would be destroyed through impoverishment. Marx assumed that as commodity production and merchant-usurer's capital tightened its grip on the countryside, the peasantry would be progressively squeezed until they were forced into the ranks of the proletariat.

The agrarian question in our country is much more complicated than the European cases which Marx analysed. There was limited growth of classes in precolonial society compared to medieval feudal society. Even after the inception of colonial capitalism, it is peasant classes and not agrarian proletariats that numerically dominated the countryside. As Shivji

(2009a:66) states, the incomplete expropriation of the peasant producer from his/her land through the infamous system of migrant labour was a means by which the peasant family subsidized capital during the colonial period. Mines, road-building, plantations and settler farms employed men and youths, paying them bachelor wages, since the burden of repro-duction of labour power fell on the peasant women left behind. Shivji is of the view that a combination of monopoly ownership and/or control of land through the state, control over the market and deployment of extra-economic coercion enabled the colonial state to maintain and reproduce a system of superexploitation. Behind the process of what appeared as commodity exchange, there lay the process of primitive accumulation or accumulation by dispossession, similar to the primitive accumulation observed in Europe by Marx and Rosa Luxemburg.

During the post-independence, especially the neoliberal period, again according to Shivji (2009a:66-7), the process of labour subsidizing capital continues in different forms. The peasant sector is the reservoir of cheap, seasonal, casual, forced and child labour under vari-ous disguises. Unable to survive on the land, the peasant seeks other casual activities, such as petty trading, craft making, construction, quarrying and seeking gold scraps. Shivji states that foreign researchers document and celebrate these 'multi-occupations' as diversification of incomes and the 'end of the peasantry', but it is nothing of the sort. Rather, these are survival strategies, meaning that peasant labour super-exploits itself through labour inten-sification.

Karl Kautsky and Lenin (drawing on Marx) thought that what was important in the en-tire analysis of the peasantry and peasant economy was differentiation based on capital accu-mulation. Forster and Maghimbi (1992:viii), citing Kautsky ([1899] 1988) and Lenin ([1899] 1956), stipulate that once capitalist relations enter agriculture, the peasantry divides itself into rich, middle and poor. The rich peasants or *kulaks* are peasant capitalists or the peasant bourgeoisie. They have started accumulating capital and are able to hire labour or machinery and obtain better seeds, animals and other inputs. Rich peasants ultimately become agrarian capitalists. The poor peasants are those who have been partly expropriated in the course of growing capitalist/market relations: they can no longer survive on farming alone. They reproduce by combining farming with selling their labour power. As capitalist agriculture grows, they are absorbed more and more into the working class. In the countryside, they be-come agricultural labourers for the rich peasants and other capitalists, and some migrate to join the urban classes. The middle peasants are the rural equivalent of the petty bourgeoisie and, being a transitional class, they get absorbed into the other two ranks as capitalist/com-mercial farming grows. For Kautsky and Lenin, what was important was to analyse capitalist relations in the peasant economy. After the failure of socialist agriculture, the analysis of capitalist agriculture is theoretically (and for policy purposes) even more important.

Although one can argue that in Tanzania (or Tanganyika then) there was no such inten-sification of differentiation within the peasantry and that the poor peasantry formed the highly exploited class, the situation confirms what Luxemburg claimed ([1913] 1951:27). She argued that, apart from the profits earned on capital actually invested in the new ter-ritories, great capital gains were made simply by acquiring land and other natural resources. As already noted, the labour to work on these natural resources was provided by the local dispossessed peasantry or by migrants from the centres of capitalism. Investment in equip-ment for the peasants' use was more profitable than in that operated by home labour, partly because the wretched condition of colonial workers made the rate of exploitation higher, but mainly because they were on the spot and could turn the natural resources seized by the capitalists into the means of production.

Alexander Chayanov (1888–1939) is another great theorist of the peasant and agrarian questions. Chayanov (1966 [1925]) offered a principal challenge to Lenin by trying to demonstrate that the agricultural statistics used by Lenin did not demonstrate irreversible capitalist class polarization, and he argued that the peasantry could play a significant role in the future socialist society supposedly being built in the Soviet Union. His disagreement with Lenin had important political implications, since he argued that peasants should be helped to prosper and modernize as individual family farmers through the establishment of cooperatives, and should not be seen as the class enemies of the (still very small) Russian urban proletariat.

According to Chayanov, the basic principle for understanding the peasant economy was the balance between the household member as a labourer and as a consumer. Peasant households and their members could either increase the number of hours they worked, or work more intensively, or sometimes both. The calculation made by households whether to work more or not was subjective, based on an estimate of how much production was needed for survival (consumption) and how much was desired for investment to increase the family's productive potential. Those estimates were balanced against the unattractiveness of agricultural labour. Households sought to reach equilibrium between production increases and the disutility of increased labour. In short, households increased their production as long as production gains outweighed the negative aspects of increased labour.

Different from Lenin, who attempted to develop a theory of 'peasantry differentiation by social class', Chayanov through his ideas gave rise to what can be termed 'a theory of demographic differentiation'. Analysing Chayanov's arguments, one can notice his position that small-scale production in household units can survive under capitalist development and that it is also possible to integrate household producers into economic structures other than capitalist ones, for example, cooperatives. In some ways, Chayanov's views can be applied to Tanzania, although one needs to be careful with the way he differentiates economic structures from capitalist ones. Various scholars in Tanzania, drawing on the Marxian tradition on the agrarian question and the peasantry (including Shivji), have reiterated that following the colonial heritage, the drawing off of the surplus from the peasantry will have the effect of preventing agrarian capitalism from developing. Thus, the upper levels of the peasantry could be expected to move into commercial and merchant activities rather than become capitalist farmers. They see recent economic changes as leading to a classical, colonial agrarian economy rather than agrarian capitalism, and therefore advocate a nationally integrated economy with an emphasis on internal consumption and on democratic cooperative peasant organizations that control both production and marketing.

Theodor Shanin is another theorist who put forth an argument that pre- and post-revolutionary Russian peasant households typically had very limited resources of land, labour and farm equipment, and even more limited money savings and access to credit. According to Shanin (1971), Russian climatic conditions made harvests very variable from year to year, and market prices for the peasants' grain fluctuated widely. For him, various policies that the Tsarist and the early Bolshevik state adopted to promote Russia's industrialization had a very damaging effect on peasant incomes, because they led to price rises for things Russian peasants bought on the market without a corresponding increase in the price of the grain they sold to raise cash. Shanin argues that the effect of all the problems facing peasant farmers was to make individual family farms very vulnerable to crisis. It was largely a matter of luck if an individual middle peasant family prospered and became a kulak household, or a poor family made it into the middle peasantry. Furthermore, a family's luck might change, and even rich peasant households would have large numbers of children, so that the family's 'capital' would have to be divided among the next generation. Rich families tended to move downwards too. So tendencies towards class polarization were offset by these multidirectional cyclical tendencies, these movements up and down. In the end, class polarization was limited by the fragility of the Russian peasant economy, that is, the unfavourable conditions facing all peasant producers.

Shanin's arguments rest on his belief that it was not really possible for peasants to succeed in sustaining accumulation of capital in the long term. Nevertheless, he does not reject the idea that *kulaks* were trying to accumulate wealth. He argues that in Russia it was certainly true there were rich peasants and poor peasants: the controversy was simply about whether the existence of differences in wealth within peasant communities was the inevitable basis for a longer-term transition to a totally different type of rural society, in which there would no longer be any 'middle peasants'. Shanin suggests that this was not really happening, because most of the rich peasant families tended to suffer a decline in economic fortunes in the fullness of time, while poor peasant households tended to recover their position and become middle peasants again. So this 'multidirectional' pattern of social mobility militated against Lenin's predicted internal transformation of the peasantry into capitalist agriculture through irreversible peasant differentiation.

Contemporary debates on the agrarian question involve scholars such as Henry Bernstein, Philip McMichael and Alain De Janvry. Bernstein, for example, examines the diverse ways in which capital and the colonial state incorporated rural producers into the production and consumption of commodities as the means of securing their own subsistence. He believes that regulations, services and the monopoly of crop producers have been used to require an often recalcitrant peasantry to organize production to meet the demands of international capital and the local state for particular commodities, trading profits, revenues and foreign exchange. For Bernstein (1977:60), the peasantry must be analysed in its relations with capital and the state in varying concrete conditions, which means within capitalist relations of production. These are mediated not through wage relations, but through various forms of household production by producers who are not fully expropriated, and who are engaged in a struggle with capital/state for effective possession and control of the conditions of production.

In his thesis, *Notes on State and Peasantry: The Tanzanian Case*, Bernstein overtly argues that what is at issue in relations between the state and the peasantry is that component of the peasant labour product that is realized through exchange, and realized through mechanisms of exchange that the state is able to control and derive revenue from. He states that given the combination of the limits of an agriculture based largely on household production, on the one hand, and the rapidly escalating costs of an expanding state on the other (together with limited, and often negative returns from other sectors of the state economy), increasing pressure by the state on the peasantry is a predictable outcome. This is manifested in the first place in the extension of state control over the conditions of exchange, charted in the institutional development of a kind of monopolistic state merchant capital (the operations of crop and transport parastatals, the annual setting of pan-territorial prices for all major crops, as well as growing monopolization by the state of the supply of peasant means of production and 'wage goods'). Resistance by peasants to the decline in the terms of trade for agricultural commodities (through 'withdrawal' from commodity production, smuggling and other forms of illicit marketing), along with limitations to further commoditization at the level of production, contributes to the stagnation of marketed output, thus intensifying the fiscal problems of the state. At this juncture, for Bernstein, the momentum of the process of state expansion and the objective need to finance it moves from attempted monopolization of that part of the peasant labour *product* that is realized through exchange, to *the attempt to control the conditions of existence and uses of peasant labour itself*. He establishes that the rationale now is to increase the absolute size of peasant output and the proportion of it that is marketed (Bernstein 1981:56).

The current state of the agrarian sector in Tanzania, especially from the Structural Adjustment Programmes (SAPs) in the 1980s through to neoliberal policies, is well captured in a later publication by Bernstein (2005:80-1). He demonstrates that the general thrust of Structural Adjustment Lending (SAL) in agriculture is, of course, to encourage agricultural export in line with the 'comparative advantage' of African economies (and their resource and factor endowments) in international trade, so as to revive the engine of economic growth and restore and maintain macroeconomic stability. Citing Friedmann (1993), Bernstein states that juxtaposed (rather than integrated) with this 'export platform' strategy of agricultural revival and productivity and income growth is the concern with environmental degradation and conservation, which assumed a centrality from the 1980s onwards comparable to that of the 1930s to 1950s, but now also linked to discourses of food security, rural poverty and livelihoods. What Bernstein tries to put forth here is consistent with ongoing measures to displace some peasants, pastoralists and local communities in the name of conservation and to label these groups as 'agents of environmental degradation'. The end result of all this is perpetuation of the agrarian crisis, to be covered in subsequent sections.

For McMichael (1997:640), decolonization (as an extension of the state system and its neocolonial framework) has significantly altered the social landscape of agriculture on a global scale. He argues that developmentalism embodies the contradictory principles of replication and substitution, and that Third World states have sought to replicate the metropolitan model, with tropical exports underwriting construction of a basic grains farm sector rooted in green revolution technologies. At the same time, land reform has been deployed to stabilize the peasantry as petty commodity producers incorporated into the national project (but also into the uncertainty of credit and commodity circuits). McMichael states that continuing agro-industrialization has resulted in a dynamic of substitution: displacing tropical exports and converting basic food cropping into commercial cropping to provide agro-industrial inputs and luxury foods for affluent urban and foreign diets. On a world scale, he believes, a new division of agricultural labour is evolving, pivoted on a complementary specialization in high-value 'non-traditional' exports from the South and low-value cereals exports from the North, reinforcing Southern food dependency. The apparent comparative advantages in this relationship have come to inform multilateral policies of 'structural adjustment' and the visions of the global regulators, the proponents of a corporate-based General Agreement on Tariffs and Trade (GATT) regime. Citing Little and Watts (1994) and Glover and Lim (1992), McMichael shows that at the base of this edifice stands the remaining peasantry, threatened with direct expulsion from the land, or transformation into contract labour for agribusiness firms (which, in regions of rapid economic growth, such as Thailand and Malaysia, is proving to be impermanent). In this manner, national developmentalism has served to intensify global integration, whose impact is also witnessed in the agrarian sector.

McMichael advocates a rethinking of the agrarian question (1984)[1] by arguing that the classical agrarian question concerned the political consequences of the subordination of landed property to capital within a problematic that assigns rural society a declining importance. For him, if we reconceptualize the agrarian transition within a world-historical context, the problematic becomes more complex. Thus, the classical nation/class problematic is contextualized, and becomes increasingly residual in (or at least subordinate to) an emerging global/peasant problematic. Neither the assumption of linearity in capital's subordination of landed property, nor the assumption that the assault on rural cultures is inevitable or desirable, is sustainable. The political counter-movement – in both proliferating social movements and in the declining legitimacy of 'developmentalism' – is generating alternative paradigms (however utopian) that acknowledge the destabilizing impact of rural assault, and privilege the voices and practices of those who experience the assault. What were once perceived as residual political and social phenomena – for instance, ethnicity (vs. citizenship), rurality (vs. urbanity) – have emerged as social forces and/or social calamities that necessitate the re-evaluation of national political landscapes. McMichael emphasizes that the new agrarian question is situated within this process of re-evaluation, which has a multitude of local and strategic considerations, just as it has some dramatic global considerations. He states that the protection and restoration of local and national food systems in the face of the forces of globalization is perhaps the central issue.

On the issue of local and national food systems, McMichael (2008:219) further states that the agrarian question of food inverts the original focus of the agrarian question, an agrarian transition. Rather than raising questions about the trajectory of a given narrative, the food sovereignty movement questions the narrative itself. In a sense, a mobilized peasantry is making its own history. It is 'mobilized' precisely because it cannot do this just as it pleases – its political intervention is conditioned by the historical political-economic conjuncture through which it is emboldened to act. And it is emboldened precisely because neoliberal capitalism's violent imposition of market relations, with severe social and ecological consequences across the world, is catastrophic. McMichael argues that capitalism is evidently deepening its internal contradictions, but this process is compounded by a politics of dispossession that complicates and/or transcends class analysis. For him, the commodification of natural and intellectual (*qua* social labour) relations crystallizes material

---

1. McMichael traces the formation of Australian colonial society and economy within the context of the changing fortunes of British hegemony in the 19th century world economy. He shows that Australia's transition from conservative origins as a penal colony supporting a grazier class oriented to export production, to liberal agrarian capitalism was not a simple reflex of imperial setting. Domestically, the 'agrarian question' – who should control the land and to what end? – was the central political struggle of this period, as urban-commercial forces contested the graziers' monopoly over the landed economy. Embedded in the conflict among settler classes was an international dimension involving a juxtaposition of laissez-faire and mercantilist phases of British political economy. McMichael argues that the transition from a patriarchal wool-growing colony to a liberal-nationalist form of capitalist development is best understood through a systematic analysis of the effect of the imperial politico-economic relationship on the social and political forces within 19th century Australia.

and cultural values distinct from those of the dominant economic discourse. Such values are fundamentally ecological, and concern how humans construct, understand and experience their relations of social reproduction.

Alain De Janvry's arguments in the context of Latin America reflect what has been happening in Tanzania with regard to the subordination of the peasant economy. In his popular thesis *The Agrarian Question and Reformism in Latin America*, De Janvry begins his discussion of Latin American agriculture by tracing the history of subordination of Latin American economies to the advanced countries (Spain and Portugal in the colonial era), later to the emerging European industrial powers in the 19th century and finally to the United States in the following centuries. According to De Janvry (1981), the effect of this domination on agricultural development has been to orient production towards export and small urban elites. The international demand for export crops has been overshadowing the domestic market for basic foods, resulting in a cycle in which the most dynamic agricultural development has taken place in the export and luxury goods sector, while agricultural production for the domestic market, mainly basic foods, has been consigned to the traditional peasant sector. The analysis by De Janvry informs the view of Henry Mapolu (1990) that, by the time of independence, the task of integrating the rural people into the capitalist market by the colonial powers had largely been accomplished. Socioeconomic structures had been built to ensure a more or less permanent flow of agricultural raw materials from Africa to Western Europe and North America and a firm dependence on the world market. Mapolu argues that, nevertheless, nowhere had the integration of rural peoples into the market economy been fully accomplished. Rural communities, often residing in inaccessible areas, or engaged in productive activities not easily penetrable by the cash nexus, continued to lead traditional forms of life more or less free of commodity production and exchange. In Tanzania, for instance, only in the mid-1960s did government 'discover' the small community of the Hadzabe people in Arusha region.

Although the situation in Latin America, whose population is nearly twice as urbanized, might differ from that of Tanzania, still the pattern of Latin American agriculture, dubbed 'functional dualism' by De Janvry, typifies some areas in our context. For De Janvry, the term 'dualism' refers to the dichotomy between the advanced capitalist production of export, industrial and luxury crops and the more traditional peasant production of domestic food crops. He uses the term 'functional' to refer to the nature of that seemingly inefficient dichotomy, identifying the essential role it plays in most Latin American economies. There are two ways in which it is functional, according to De Janvry. The first is through the peasant sector's overexploitation of its own family labour, which provides relatively cheap food products for the domestic markets, because of the small size of the market and state policies that favour industry and export-oriented agriculture. Second, the present-day Latin American peasant family typically has one or more of its members doing wage work to supplement the inadequate production on its land. Such workers make up the so-called semi-proletariat, whose wage income is supplemented by its families' subsistence food production.

AFRICAN PERSPECTIVES ON THE AGRARIAN QUESTION

The classical agrarian question was concerned with the transition to capitalism, both within agriculture and in the mechanisms through which agricultural development contributes to industrialization. The agrarian question of capital is resolved when transitions to capitalist agriculture and industry are complete (Bernstein 1996; Byres 1991). But there is not just one pathway through this transition – both its character and the outcomes are shaped by class relations and struggles, depending on the strength of contending interests of landed property and agrarian capital, agricultural labour in a variety of forms (including tenant peasants) and emerging industrial capital. State policies and interventions also influence agrarian transformation. Byres (1991), following Lenin, describes two broad alternative pathways: (a) 'accumulation from above', the Prussian or *Junker* path, in which precapitalist land owners are transformed into agrarian capitalists. This occurred in parts of Latin America, northern India and South Africa, as well as in 19th century Germany; (b) 'accumulation from below', or the American path, where conditions for petty commodity production are established and a fully capitalist agriculture emerges through class differentiation of peasants and other kinds of small producers.

Much attention has been given to African agricultural transformation, albeit with limited results (see Mkandawire and Soludo 1999; Mafeje 2003; Moyo and Yeros 2007; Moyo 2008; Bernstein 2002 and 2005; Rukuni et al. 2006; AGRA 2007). As discussed by several authors (see, for example, Bernstein 2002; Byres 1991 and 1996) the classical agrarian question in Africa was concerned with the transition from feudal or other type of agrarian society to capitalist or industrial society, through the transformation of the role of various agrarian classes (different peasant classes, agricultural workers, landowners, wider capital) in struggles for democracy and socialism. This also went hand in hand with the transformation of the social relations of production and development of the productive forces in agriculture and agriculture's contribution to the accumulation of capital resources, on a classic transition towards the capitalist mode of production. Recent debates on the land and agrarian questions query the relevance of land reform in the current context of globalization and the global demand for alternative and clean energy sources. The recent experience in Zimbabwe, though viewed as a politically 'contrived' reform, has been caused by uneven development and the manipulation of 'Northern' markets and SAPs, which have depressed agricultural production and prices in the 'South'. Intense land questions and resistance to neoliberalism have re-emerged in land struggles, led by new social movements (Petras and Veltmeyer 2001; Ghimire 2001; Moyo 2001 and Yeros 2002 quoted in Moyo and Yeros 2007). Bernstein (2002) argued that the agrarian question in the 'North' had been resolved, which heralded the end of the 'classic' land and agrarian reforms, except in isolated parts of the South. The socioeconomic destruction of peasantries and their limited capacity to struggle for land redistribution in Africa is considered to constrain the potential for popular land reforms. Tanzania is an interesting case, because here peasants still own much of the farmland. There was less alienation compared to the settler colonies.

Earlier debates on the agrarian question in Africa lamented the cooption of Africa's petty-bourgeois ruling class as an obstacle to reform (Fanon 1967). However, some of the later authors were more optimistic (see, for example, Cabral 1979). Shivji (1976) argued that the socialistic posturing masked the emergence of a 'bureaucratic bourgeoisie', which reproduced peripheral capitalism. Since structural adjustment, the African state has retreated further from agrarian interventions, giving leadership to markets which, in the event, were not as well established as had been expected, and whose 'informality' grew further (Mkandawire and Soludo 1999). The result was the same: a failed agrarian transition.

A more recent debate in Africa has moved into the issues of democratic states and development in relation to agrarian reform. The emphasis is on the importance of autonomous policy space, with an apparent consensus that development requires autonomy, and that autonomy requires a new conciliatory foundation, a 'people's contract', together with effective planning bureaucracies (Edigheji 2006; Moyo and Yeros 2007). As argued in Moyo and Yeros (2007), the underlying challenge of implementing agrarian reform remains the securing of the requisite autonomy (willingness and orientation) and capacity of the state to effect the desired policies, together with the effective mobilization of popular social forces in support of the envisioned agrarian (structural) reforms. The debate has expanded further to encompass the issue of capacity required by the state, without distinguishing 'state apparatus' from 'state power', understating the fact that the state apparatus does not have power of its own, and that its exercise of state power reflects the correlation of class forces at any given time (Callaghy 1988; Hyden and Bratton 1992; Moyo and Yeros 2007). For instance, much of the South African debate on land and agrarian reform (see, for example, Hall 2007) focused on the failings of land and agriculture departments (as one part of the executive), without examining the other branches of the state apparatus (judiciary, security, etc.), let alone pursuing a (socialist) class analysis of the political forces that define state power. Yet, agrarian reform would impact and alter the correlation of class forces, to the extent of creating a disjuncture between the state apparatus and state power (Moyo and Yeros 2007).

The nature of Africa's current intellectual and policy debates on land reflects important ideological and political contestations over the definition of its land and agrarian questions, and hence the trajectory of the land and agrarian reform that is required to undergird sustainable development, and the role of the state vis-à-vis domestic markets (including agrarian markets – land, labour and capital) and international markets. The neoliberal agenda emphasizes market liberalization within a global hegemonic project, which subordinates the African nation state accumulation project to global financial capital. The contradictions in this neoliberal trajectory manifest themselves partly in Africa's land and agrarian questions, ineffective land reforms and the mobilization of various social forces over land.

It is important to note that central to classic analyses within this tradition have been (grand) theories of class formation within 'transitions to capitalism' in agriculture, with a particular emphasis on the (assumed) proletarianization of the peasantry in relation to processes of industrial transformation. Importantly, this tradition has paid close attention to patterns of commodification of peasant production and processes of accumulation in colonial and independent Africa, as well as to "... household forms, agrarian labor processes, technical change, rural labor markets, patterns of migration and demography, processes of class differentiation in the countryside and rural politics" (Bernstein and Byers 2001:37). While acknowledging all of this as critical to understandings of agrarian change, it is important to emphasize some of the limitations of a strictly materialist approach, which ignored the many symbolic and discursive dimensions to agrarian relations and politics and assumed the inevitability of proletarianization and the false dichotomy between rural and urban domains.

Under capitalism, the peasantry remains in a state of flux, as proletarianization coexists with peasantization and semi-proletarianization. Under structural adjustment, African peasants have continued as always to be "multi-occupational, straddling urban and rural residences, [and] flooding labor markets" (Bryceson 2000). This process has been accompanied by intensified migration and high urbanization (3.5 per cent growth annually, and 40 per cent of the population), in spite of deindustrialization and retrenchments around the continent, suggesting that African countries could be characterized by high urban unemployment. The transition to capitalism in settler Africa occurs through disarticulated accumulation subordinated to the needs of the centre (Moyo and Yeros 2004b). It can be noted that, despite growing urbanization on the African continent, the vast majority of Africans are still located in, connected to or are dependent in multiple ways on their relationships with rural or agrarian environments. Secondly, major global changes over the past few decades, such as the hegemony of neoliberalism, the HIV/AIDS pandemic, as well as new global movements, have generated new kinds of agrarian dynamics and relationships on the African continent that need to be closely examined and better understood.

Agrarian Change and Socioeconomic Transformation in Africa

Based on the nature and form of control of state power and the ideological groundings of the ruling incumbents, national development strategies and the purpose of land and agrarian reforms have become convoluted. Agrarian reform was always understood to serve national industrialization and development and continues to have this potential, although recent debates underplay it (Fernandes 2001). There are generally three views on the purpose of agrarian reform: the 'social', the 'economic' and the 'political', all underlain by questions of social justice (AIAS Mimeo).[2] The social version emphasizes a welfarist focus, which aims to redistribute some land to the poor, alongside maintenance of the large 'modern farm sector'. The economic version argues for promoting redistribution towards developing efficient small commercial farmers to create employment and multiplier effects, which integrate the home market. The political version argues for challenging the political power of the landed and transforming the entire agrarian structure as a basis for an introverted development strategy. These diverse versions of the purpose and approach to land reform can combine in various forms, depending on the specific political and economic conditions of nations over time.

A 'merchant path', comprising a variety of urban [petty-] bourgeois elements with access to land, farming on a medium scale but integrated into export markets and global agroindustry, is gradually emerging in some countries (AIAS Mimeo).[3] A richer class of peasants has emerged alongside the semi-proletarianized and landless, while full proletarianization was generally forestalled, not least by state action. A limited 'middle-to-rich peasant path' of petty-commodity producers was created through rural differentiation and active state policies of land access and tenure, but subjected to contradictory agrarian policies, which under land market reform and neoliberalism have been restrictive.

A 'rural poor path', including fully proletarianized and semi-proletarianized peasants,

---

2. For more detailed information and debate on this matter see Chrispen Sukume and Sam Moyo (2003), *Farm Sizes, Decongestion and Land Use: Implications of the Fast Track Land Redistribution Programme in Zimbabwe*, AIAS Mimeo; Sam Moyo (2003) *Land Redistribution: Allocation and Beneficiaries*, AIAS Mimeo; and Sam Moyo and Prosper Matondi (2003), *Agricultural Production Targets*, AIAS Mimeo.

3. Ibid.

has also occurred and is characterized by the contradictory tendencies of full proletarianization (under economic and demographic pressure) and retention/acquisition of a family plot for petty-commodity production and social security (consistent with functional dualism). These poor migrate from rural areas to urban centres, across international boundaries and participate in the informal economic sector, both rural and urban, while struggling for re-peasantization, sometimes successfully.

'Poverty reduction' and 'integrated rural development' strategies seek to bolster functional dualism in its moment of crisis (Moyo and Yeros 2007): structural adjustment has led to the abandonment of the development agenda. Direct and indirect political action and social catastrophes have brought back land reform (Moyo and Yeros 2007). Development strategy entailed economic and agrarian policies that direct the use of land for extroverted (export) purposes, rather than for developing the national market and related industries, while favouring distorted accumulation by a small elite and foreign capital (Moyo 2004), leading to underconsumption and mass unemployment. These policies repressed agricultural productivity among the peasantry, leading to depressed wages and peasant incomes. In addition, liberalization led to the conversion of large tracts of farming land to exclusively wildlife and nature-based land uses under even larger scale 'conservancies'.

The World Development Report (2008) highlights the need for a green revolution in sub-Saharan Africa. With many countries in sub-Saharan Africa, and Tanzania in particular, gearing up for the green revolution, there is likely to be a re-engineering of the traditional agricultural sector into a modernized vehicle of economic growth. If care is not taken, this will mean that there will be little place left for traditional smallholder agriculture. The majority of government officials and policymakers support more modest development plans in the agricultural sector. The focus in the early stages should be on agricultural growth and development, in addition to the extension of the service sector driven by local demand. The agricultural sector now is at the forefront of Tanzania's development agenda, especially with the launch of the *Kilimo Kwanza* (Agriculture First)[4] campaign in July 2009 (URT 2009).

We thus approach a paradox: in the midst of such widespread crises of production and reproduction, partly manifested in 'the shrinkage of the peasant sector', combined with increasing differentiation between those able and unable to farm as a significant basis of their reproduction, there seems to be mounting tension over land ownership. A wide range of recent evidence concerning competition for land, and the conflicts it generates, is presented by Pauline Peters (2004), who distinguishes the various types of agents in and strands of this process as follows

1. "growing populations and movements of people looking for better/more land or fleeing civil disturbances";
2. "rural groups seek to intensify commodity production and food production while retrenched members of a downsized salariat look for land to improve food and income options";
3. "states demarcate forestry and other reserves, and identify areas worthy of conservation (often under pressure from donors and international lobbying groups)";
4. "representatives of the state and political elites appropriate land through means ranging from the questionable to the illegal"; and

---

4. More discussion of this is provided in Part C of the paper.

5.   "valuable resources both on and under the land (timber, oil, gold, other minerals) attract intensifying exploitation by agents from the most local (unemployed youth or erstwhile farmers seeking ways to obtain cash) to transnational networks (of multinational corporations, foreign governments and representatives of African states)…" (2004:291).

The other side of this coin is the growing number of those who are too poor to farm, even if they are able to assert claims to land. This undermines the assumption linking the two parts of Sara Berry's observation that *"most people in rural areas have access to land, and are therefore able to cultivate on their own account"* (1993:135). Indeed, in an important sense that bears on empirical fieldwork and its findings, those too poor to cultivate on their own account often tend to go 'missing', even when they supply rural labour markets which, as just noted, are typically a condition of small-scale, as well as larger-scale, agrarian petty commodity production. As noted in Anderson and Broch-Due (1999), those who do not farm or farm only in the most marginal ways, even if they have claims to land, are effectively landless and may well disappear from surveys of farming populations. There is a nice expression of this in the Maasai notion that 'the poor are not us,' that is, those without cattle in a pastoralist society become by definition non-pastoralists. This is a discursive manoeuvre with a heavy normative charge and serious implications for such key aspects of moral economy as identity, inclusion and the 'politics of belonging' (Kuba and Lentz 2006). The situation, then, is one of growing numbers in the countryside, or spanning rural areas (and different rural areas) and towns, who now depend – directly *and indirectly* – on the sale of their labour power for their own daily reproduction. Moreover, this is an effect of class differentiation in the countryside, even when it is not matched by the formation of large-scale landed property/ agrarian capital at the other end of the class spectrum.

The Dynamics of Land Tenure Systems in Africa

The escalation since 2000 of the land conflict in Zimbabwe is but one of many struggles for land reform and reparations that reflect the failure of the state to address the land and development nexus on the continent. The land question in Africa is indeed a by-product of globalized control of land, natural and mineral resources, not least as a mirror of the incomplete decolonization processes in ex-settler colonies, but also because of the pursuit of foreign 'investment' in a neoliberal framework, which has marginalized the rural poor. Global financial capital is increasingly entangled in conflicts over land, minerals and natural resources in various rich African enclaves, highlighting the external dimension of distorted development.

In essence, the distortion of land property relations, including issues of land concentration and exclusion, the expansion of private landed property and the deepening of extroverted capitalist relations of agrarian production in the context of food insecurity, increased food imports (and aid dependence), the continued decline of the value of growing agrarian exports and the collapse of Africa's nascent agro-industrial base, define the significance of land in the political economy of African development. The agrarian question of capital, however, is only one side of the coin: on the other side, the agrarian question *of the dispossessed* (or of labour) has not yet been resolved. Structural unemployment, poverty, food insecurity, land hunger and continued rule by tyrants mean that the struggle for democracy and against oppression and exploitation continues. The agenda of the incomplete agrarian question is contesting the monopolistic privileges of white/corporate farming, and of chiefly/bureaucratic elites in former 'homelands', and creating the conditions for more diverse forms of commodity production, that is, 'accumulation from below' – always recognizing that this will involve processes of class differentiation.

The 'crisis of African agriculture' – in terms of production (and productivity), income, contributions to reproduction and any possibility of profit – is not distributed equally across the social categories that farm or otherwise have an interest in farming and access to land. Some of those with recognized claims on land are too poor to farm: they lack capital to secure inputs or command over labour through the social relations of kinship – typically mediated by patriarchal relations of gender and generation – or markets, and/or access to credit that is affordable and timely. On the other hand, those able to reproduce relatively robust agricultural petty commodity enterprises, and *a fortiori* to expand the scale of their farming, typically do so with reproduction/investment funds derived from wage employment (and also from trade and transport).

The African land question is an element of the agrarian question and has some unique social features and approaches to land reform, including how the dominant emphasis on land tenure reform has evolved. The first, primary difference of African land tenure systems, according to Mafeje (2003), is the absence at the advent of African colonization of widespread purely feudal political formations, based on the specific social relations of production in which land and labour processes are founded on serfdom or its variants under feudal or even semi-feudal landlords. Essentially, the extraction of surplus value from serfs by landlords through ground rents using primitive forms of land rental allotments and through the mandatory provision of different forms of 'bonded' or 'unfree' labour services, sharecropping and other tributary extractions on the peasantry under feudalism, was not widespread in Africa. Instead, as pointed out by Mafeje (2003), most rural African societies were structured around lineage based 'communal' structures of political authority and social organization, in which access to land was founded on recognized and universal usufruct rights allocated to families (both pastoral and sedentary) of members of given lineage groupings (Moyo 2004). Such land rights also included those eventually allocated to assimilated 'slaves', migrants and settlers, as Mamdani (2001) and other scholars argue.

This means that African 'households' held land and mobilized their labour relations in production processes relatively autonomously from the ruling lineages and 'chiefs', mainly for their own consumption needs and secondarily for social or 'communal' projects on a minor scale. Under these conditions, production for trade, generally considered to have been long distance in nature, has occurred on a small but increasing scale since colonialism (Moyo 2004). Amin (1972) has argued that these African social formations had some exploitative elements of tributary social relations of production. These can be adduced from the contributions that households made, from small parts of the household product, to labour, to the rulers' and social projects (e.g., the king's fields and granary reserves). But, the essential issue that distinguishes the African land question is the absence of widespread rural social relations of production based on serfdom, such as land renting and bonded labour, in a context where there was monopoly over land by a few landlords. Colonialism extended the extroversion of production and the process of surplus value extraction through the control of markets and 'extra-economic' force, but left the *land and labour relations generically 'free'*. The exception to this was in settler Africa (Moyo 2004) and feudal Ethiopia.

Commodification of farming and labour power was not matched, to the same degree, by the evident commodification of land. Dispossession and land alienation, of course, was the key to the economies of colonies of European settlement (South Africa, the Rhodesias and Kenya), which were inextricably bound up with the formation of labour reserves to supply mines, settler farms and plantations. They were also significant in other kinds of colonies through concessions for mining, timber extraction and for government purposes, including infrastructure (dams, ports, railways, official buildings) and indeed 'protected' (conservation) areas.

However, dispossession was the exception rather than the norm. More typical was the administration of 'customary law', including 'communal land tenure', placed in the hands of chiefs and headmen under indirect rule. While this approach was justified as respecting African 'tradition', in practice it departed radically from African experience, as it was inevitably 'territorialized'. Colonial officials, steeped in European conceptions of jurisdiction, sought to fix the boundaries of 'tribal' areas and 'communal land', to measure and map the spaces they enclosed and to regulate the uses to which they were put. This process was widely contested and frustrated and often remained incomplete. It provided one important arena of the operation of 'multiple regimes of authority' and its ambiguities, giving rise to increased and less overt and vigorous clashes between 'native authorities' and colonial states; between rival claimants to 'traditional authority' (and their followers); between those claiming rights to land as members of 'communities of descent' and 'strangers'; and sometimes along lines of gender division (Chimhowu and Woodhouse 2006).

At the same time – and a third generalization with its attendant variations – there is a kind of scissors effect at work for those in rural Africa (the great majority), whose reproduction is secured through combinations of own farming and off-farm wages and self-employment, including the many whose off-farm income has been essential, historically, to meeting the entry and reproduction costs of their farming enterprises. In Tanzania and many other countries in the region, for example, there is also growing evidence of shortages of arable land and often grazing land, especially in areas of better soils, wetlands and/or transport links to urban markets, as a result of various combinations of intensified pressures on reproduction (with effects for patterns of commodification) and demographic concentration, including in-migration to more favoured farming areas (Woodhouse et al. 2000; Peters 2004).

The social perspective of the role of agriculture in development emphasizes the importance of ensuring the availability and accessibility of basic food and wage-goods for consumption by the majority of working peoples. Equitable access to and control of land, labour and agrarian resources, and state support particularly for small producers, are considered critical to reversing the social costs of human deprivation arising from food insecurity, and to achieving food sovereignty.

Land reform is a fundamental dimension of the agrarian question, and the agrarian question in turn is central to addressing the national question. It has also to be noted that land reform is a necessary but not sufficient condition for national development, including the productivity deficits of agriculture (Moyo and Yeros 2007). The land question in Southern African has tended to overshadow its agrarian question. Land reform tends to be posited as follows: the need to restructure the distribution of land ownership towards an envisioned 'democratic' agrarian structure, which can promote social, economic and political transformation; enhancing the security of land tenure for all (particularly the poor), through a legally enforceable system of property rights, which does not necessarily imply private property; and a reorientation of the purpose and effectiveness of land utilization (agricultural production patterns and systems) to satisfy the home market (Moyo 2004). From the 1980s, under the influence of international finance and neoliberal economics, state-led and interventionist land reform was removed from the development agenda and replaced by market-based land policies in pursuit of the privatization of land and market-based land transfers. This led to the abandonment of the project of integrating agriculture and industry on a national basis and the promotion instead of their integration into global markets. It resulted in decreased economic and social security, intensified migration to urban areas and deepening underdevelopment (Moyo and Yeros 2004). But when agrarian reform (including land reform) is not implemented, the landless and other classes and social groups tend to intensify their struggle for land (for both social reproduction and wealth accumulation) through strategies intended to force governments to implement redistributive land reforms (Fernandes 2001). Thus, land reform is generally critical to addressing a variety of economic and political inequities and exclusions that shape the national question, within specific national conditions.

The control of land has increasingly become a key source for mobilizing power through electoral politics in which capital and class power direct struggles for democratization and development. Land reforms can be critical sites of electoral political struggles, when class and race power-structures in relation to the interests of external capital are unevenly matched in the context of unequal land distribution, as the Zimbabwe experience shows. In the 2007 Kenya general elections and several others in the past, the outcome was grounded in violent strategies to maintain power by politicians, who manipulated longstanding but latent interethnic disputes over land. Thus, the nature and form of control of state power and the ideological groundings of the ruling incumbents can be critical to the form and content of land reforms.

THE AGRARIAN QUESTION IN TANZANIA

The agrarian sector in Tanzania, as in many other developing countries where the majority of the population depend entirely on land for their livelihoods, is in crisis. Primarily, this crisis has been instigated by neoliberal economic reforms in the past decades and has intensified through the continuing forms of accumulation of capital, leaving most of local communities in a state of destitution and impoverishment, while exposing them to what can be termed massive exploitation and marginalization. This state of affairs indicates a pervasive agrarian crisis. This third part integrates various approaches to explain and discuss the agrarian question in Tanzania. This is a complex phenomenon, which needs the use of various disciplines in analysis, including political economy, sociology, economics, history, political theory and anthropology.

Historical Perspectives on the Agrarian Question

According to McMichael (2007:31), in the classical conception, the agrarian question was to be resolved by capital through particular class transformation processes and political alliances within each nation state. This state-centric view discounted the role of imperialist relations during the era in which the agrarian question emerged. McMichael is of the view that postcolonial states, with few exceptions (including Tanzania and China) constructed in the Western image, adapted the idealized national economic development model, founded on a dynamic commercial relationship between national industrial and agricultural sectors. He states that within this framework, green revolution technology was transferred to the Third World to modernize its farm sectors by constructing a capitalist farming class to provide urban classes with food.

Colonial Phase

Suffice it to note that an adequate analysis of the agrarian question in Tanzania should be traced within the colonial economy and the resultant efforts to integrate the country into the metropolitan capitalist structures. Shivji (1975:10-11), for example, argues that the development of agrarian capitalism in Tanganyika has to be distinguished from the kind of capitalist development in the European countries that Marx described. He argues that, taken historically, the development of capitalism and widespread commodity exchange in the now developed capitalist countries was no doubt progressive, both as an opposition to the previous mode (feudalism) and because it revolutionized the very process of production, thereby enabling the development of the productive forces by leaps and bounds. The author states that this increase in overall productivity freed labour from the land to work in the factories. In sum, it proletarianized the peasantry, something which was (and is) precisely not the case in Africa because of the very historical situation under which capitalism came to Africa and the nature of the continent's contemporary relations with developed capitalist countries.

Shivji and many others argue that the agrarian question has its roots in the appropriation of land and the entire changes to land tenure systems in Tanzania since the colonial era. The Presidential Commission Report (1994) demonstrates that the enactment of the famous Imperial Decree of 26 November 1895 instituted the philosophy of land ownership under German rule, in terms of which all lands, whether occupied or not, were treated as

Crown lands. Olenasha (2005:2) states that there was, however, an exception to this general rule in situations where private persons or communities could prove ownership. Private persons could prove ownership by documentary evidence, while traditional communities could prove the same through use and occupation. This spirit has shaped and regulated matters pertaining to land tenure systems throughout British colonial rule and the postcolonial era, as will be shown in the subsequent discussion.

During British colonialism, there were a few alterations to the central principles of land tenure practised by the former colonial power, with special focus on the development of the colonial economy to facilitate the production of agricultural raw materials, while controlling and alienating indigenous land rights. The Land Ordinance of 1923 (No. 3) for example, declared all lands to be public lands. Shivji (1998:2) holds that this ordinance is still the prime basis of the land tenure regime, and it sought to become this by declaring and defining customary tenure without securing and statutorily entrenching customary titles and rights, and by authorizing the governor to make land grants in the form of temporally limited rights of occupancy. This meant in practice the alienation of indigenous lands to settlers and foreign corporations, and preserving the overarching control of the state over land by vesting the radical title in the state, which in turn was legitimized by the hortatory provision that land "shall be held and administered for the use and economic benefit, direct or indirect, of the natives of the Territory".

In 1928, there was a major change in the land tenure regime when the Land Ordinance was amended to expand the meaning of the right of occupancy to recognize customary law titles. In terms of the Land Ordinance (Amendment) 1928 (No. 7), the governor was authorized to make grants of land in the form of 'rights of occupancy' for periods of up to 99 years (this is also the case with the current Land Act). It is said that this Land Ordinance was the tenure under which the colonial state alienated the public lands occupied by indigenous natives to non-natives, including immigrant communities and foreign companies. Olenasha (2005:5) argues that the effect of declaring land to be public land does not have a sufficient explanation in law and it would seem to have been just an administrative tactic to legitimize the dispossession of Africans of their lands. He is of the view that because lands are public and, further, because customary titles to land do not enjoy the same status as granted rights of occupancy, the British colonial state could implement its economic objectives without impediment. Merging property and sovereignty in land through the exercise of radical title was the best way to exploit and plunder the natural resources of the Tanganyika colony. It was also to exacerbate the challenges facing the traditional economy and intensify the agrarian crisis.

After the Second World War, British colonial rule concentrated profoundly on the exploitation of colonial resources in order to reconstruct Britain's wounded economy. This led to the use of force in the production of cash crops by peasants. A government circular of 1953 (Tanganyika Government 1953) emphasized the need for indigenous people to imitate the use of modern methods of production used in non-native lands within the framework of modernization, whose intention, among other things, was to rationalize the further alienation of land to non-natives (Shivji 1998:5). The motive behind the colonial land tenure systems in Tanganyika was therefore to abolish customary land tenure and enhance a freehold system. Through this system, the indigenous peasants and pastoralists were to be alienated from their native surroundings in order to be integrated into the world capitalist economy through the production of cash crops to address the needs of the colonial power.

Post-Colonial Phase: Villagization and the Arusha Declaration

Bernstein (1981:45) notes that after independence in 1961, the newly independent state emphasized the benefits of peasants living together in nuclear villages, as opposed to the patterns of scattered settlement prevailing in most areas of Tanzania. This was the theme of Nyerere's inaugural speech as president in 1962, subsequently incorporated into the broad message of *Ujamaa* introduced with the Arusha Declaration in 1967. Bernstein shows that from 1967 to 1973, the number of those living in officially designated '*Ujamaa* villages' increased from about half a million to about two million, or 15 per cent of the rural population. The great majority had been 'mobilized' to form villages by local party and government officials, whose recourse to commandist methods is well documented. For Bernstein, of particular significance in this period was the implementation from 1969 of a number of centrally approved and highly organized 'operations' (a characteristically military metaphor of mobilization) to move the rural populations of entire districts and regions into nuclear settlements. These operations provided the prototype for the villagization on a national scale ordered at the end of 1973, and completed by 1976.

It is further stated by Shivji (1998:12) that by the end of 1973, the ruling party had grown impatient with the lack of progress and abandoned its earlier methods based on voluntarism and persuasion by making villagization compulsory. The president ordered that by the end of 1976 the whole rural population should be moved, an operation which resettled millions of peasants and pastoralists in old or newly formed villages. The Land Commission established that among the major features of the operation was the total disregard of existing customary land tenure systems as well as the fact that virtually no thought was given to the future land tenure in newly established villages (URT 1994:Vol. I, 43). Villagization and the whole operation were said to have had a major impact on both land tenure and the rights of rural land users. The result was confusion in tenure and the total undermining of security for customary landholders and, above all, the opening up of possibilities for alienation of village land on a scale greater than during colonial times (Shivji 1998:12; Tenga 1987:46)

Although the Villages and Ujamaa Villages Act 1975 (No. 21) does not provide an authority for land tenure in villages, it establishes the village assembly (a meeting of all adults in the village), a village council of approximately 25 persons, and a committee of the village council to deal with matters pertaining to land tenure. It is important to note that under the law, the power of the village assembly is very limited and that of the village council is conditional on the powers of and directions from the minister, district commissioner and district council. As already stated, the villagization programme did not provide security for village land, but rather immensely contributed to devastating the security of deemed rights for peasants and pastoral communities.

Contemporary Perspectives on the Agrarian Question

For scholars such as Araghi (1995 and 2000) and McMichael (2007), current academic debates over the contemporary agrarian question are framed by an academic reductionism shared by neoliberal and orthodox Marxist perspectives on the transience of the 'peasantry'. They argue that this perspective is governed by the lens of capital accumulation – essentially that capitalism follows a path-dependent resolution of social forms into the capital-labour relationship, and/or that 'peasants' are a historical anachronism, as scale is necessary to survive in the market or to realize the potential of 'social labour'. Such arguments subscribe to not only the nature of the colonial powers but also the state, which inherited the role of landlord, hence mediating the relationship between producers (peasants) and consumers (industrial metropolitan capital) through merchant capital.

It is noteworthy that the current land tenure regime in Tanzania is a product of colonialism. In the last one and half decades there were, however, major reforms to land tenure in Tanzania, all of which have contributed to the current agrarian question. Olenasha (2005:1) has stated that the present reforms began with the appointment and work of the highly celebrated Presidential Commission of Inquiry into Land Matters, whose work led to the formulation of the National Land Policy 1995, which paved the way for the enactment of two major pieces of legislation, the Land and Village Land Acts of 1999 (Acts No. 4 and 5 respectively) (URT 1999). In 2004 and 2008, the Land Act was amended. The establishment of the Land Bank and its administration by the Tanzania Investment Centre (TIC) is said to be one of the significant administrative developments relevant to land tenure.

The Commission, which was appointed in January 1991, was mandated to investigate the people's complaints and grievances over land and to recommend new land policy and tenure systems. Shivji (1999:1) notes that the Commission visited all the (then) 20 regions of mainland Tanzania and all districts except two, and held 277 public meetings in 145 villages and 132 urban centres. Total attendance at the meetings was estimated at around 83,000, of whom 58,000 were men and 25,000 women. Over 3,000 persons submitted complaints and opinions in public meetings, while some 800 sent written complaints. All told, the commissioners spent about 300 working days on regional tours. The transcript of the evidence collected by the Commission runs to some 4,000 pages.

The final report was in two volumes. The first deals with land policy and land tenure, while the second contains 40 case studies of major land disputes throughout the country and a summary of the letters of complaint. Both volumes were published by the Ministry of Lands, Housing and Urban Development in cooperation with the Nordic Institute of African Studies. Volume I is available, but the 300 copies of Volume II produced simultaneously are sitting in the ministry and have never been released to the public. There has been considerable public debate on the land and agrarian question in Tanzania since the Commission's report.

Shivji (1999:1) also notes that in June 1995, the Ministry of Lands published the National Land Policy, which was not released into the public domain until much later. The policy was apparently the basis of the bills drafted by a consultant hired from Britain. It is noteworthy that both the National Land Policy and the bills ignored the major recommendations of the Commission, while taking in details in an ad hoc fashion. It is argued that instead of decentralizing and democratizing land tenure management, the National Land Policy is viewed by the majority as centralizing and reinforcing state power to control land (Shivji 1995).

The Land and Village Land Acts of 1999 stipulate that all land in mainland Tanzania "shall continue to be public land and remain vested in the President as trustee for and on behalf of all citizens of Tanzania" (Cl. 4(1)). This was also the basis of the land tenure system put in place by the Land Ordinance of 1923, and proof that the Acts overtly continue the essential colonial principle of land tenure, namely integrating property with power. Moreover, as did the Land Ordinance, the Acts establish a system of rights of occupancy relating to the use and occupation of land. This means the state is the final owner of land, grants rights of occupancy and bears customary occupation and use of land. However, the

Acts acknowledge customary tenure as equivalent to granted rights of occupancy. The implication of this is that the president is given the power (as was the governor during colonial rule) to grant land to a foreigner or non-native on reserved or general land for interests proclaimed to be 'public', including investment. This is also to say that the Acts confirm foreign ownership of village lands under a long term lease under indigenous titles, whether granted or customary, hence paving the way for various forms of dispossession and displacement, as will be discussed later. All these provisions have significant impacts on land users in Tanzania, including peasants and pastoralists, and to their sources of livelihood.

According to Pallotti (2008:230) the implementation of the Village Land Act has become one of the components of the Property and Business Formalization Programme launched by the government in 2004 and popularly known as MKURABITA (*Mpango wa kurasimisha rasilimali na biashara Tanzania*).[5] Drafted by the Institute for Liberty and Democracy under the auspices of the former president, Benjamin Mkapa, this programme aims to promote the formalization of citizens' property rights in accordance with the economic model developed by Hernando de Soto, who was invited by Mkapa to address Tanzania's parliament in February 2003. Pallotti states that while the MKURABITA programme is still officially in its planning phase, a land pilot project was implemented in some villages in Handeni district (Tanga region) in late 2006, with the aim of "test[ing] ways of making titling quicker and cheaper". He adds that apart from several technical problems experienced in the implementation of the Handeni pilot project, the Legal and Human Rights Centre noted that "land grabbing became a normal habit during the titling project", and that, in spite of the Village Land Act provisions confirming land allocations made during the villagization period, land disputes and conflicts which had first emerged during villagization were exacerbated by the granting of the new title deeds.

The Ministry of Lands and Human Settlement Development commissioned a draft Strategic Plan for the Implementation of the Land Laws (SPILL), which would "streamline the land laws into the socioeconomic life of Tanzania". SPILL, which was completed in April 2005, sought to operationalize land laws, that is, do everything that needs to be done by the land administration machinery to frame and safeguard customary and granted land rights for land users. SPILL also aims to facilitate the alleviation of poverty, particularly in rural areas (URT, MLHSD 2005:4). However, according to Pallotti (2008:230), SPILL (whose implementation would cost Tshs (Tanzanian shillings) 300 bn over a ten-year period) redefines the nature of Tanzania's land tenure reform by speeding up both the decentralization of land delivery and land administration services to the districts and villages and the involvement of the private sector in implementing the land laws, while mostly paying only lip service to the need to secure villagers' land rights. SPILL mirrors the neoliberal economic development approach of the Land (Amendment) Act 2004, promoting the individualization of land rights and even acknowledging the possibility that the modernization of the agricultural sector could (or should?) create a class of landless people in rural areas.

Izumi (1999:10) argues that the economic liberalization adopted since the early 1980s seems to have further accelerated such processes, both in pace and scale, and in many contexts liberalization has opened new opportunities for investment in land, leading to increased and intensified contests over land. Quoting Moyo (1998), Izumi notes that as land gains value as an investment commodity, land-grabbing by political elites, appropriation of village

5. To be discussed in detail in subsequent sections.

land by the state and allocation of land to investors both nationally and locally have become common. On the other hand, the poor are desperately selling land to survive deepening poverty. Retrenchment, unemployment and declining real wages due to high inflation are forcing urban workers to seek rural land in order to produce food to supplement their low incomes.

Liberalization policies are said to have created the conditions that threaten to give effect to the fears of rural landholders following a number of publicly reported 'scandals' involving large-scale alienations of village lands, particularly in pastoral areas, to so-called 'investors' – foreign hunting companies, hoteliers, breeders of exotic birds, wildlife ranchers, miners of rare stones and so on (Shivji 2009b:113). This state of affairs shows that an understanding of the complexities of the political and social contradictions resulting from the colonial and postcolonial land tenure systems and the trajectories of capital accumulation within the neoliberal economy is of paramount importance in land and agrarian questions in Tanzania.

Tanzanian Peasant Exploitation and the Agrarian Question

As in many so-called 'underdeveloped countries', peasants in Tanzania are not just the leftovers of colonial and postcolonial state structures. Rather, they are the real foundation of capitalist exploitation. It is this foundation that bears existing imperialist exploitative relations and perpetuates the existence of a large peasantry and peasant forms of livelihood in the name of accumulation.

On the nature and significance of the peasantry in Africa and Latin America in particular, it is argued by Moyo and Yeros (2007:25-6) that the peasantry – small-scale/family agriculturalists operating within the generalized system of commodity production – does not constitute a class in itself, but inherent in it are the antagonistic tendencies of proletarian and proprietor. The ideal-type 'peasant household' reproduces itself as both capital and labour simultaneously and in internal contradiction, but according to Moyo and Yeros, this combination of capital and labour is not spread evenly within the peasantry for two reasons. First, the peasantry is differentiated between rich, middle and poor petty-commodity producers, a spectrum that ranges from the capitalist who employs labour-power beyond the family to the semi-proletarian who sells it. As such, the middle peasantry is the only category that embodies the ideal-type of petty-bourgeois production, managing to neither hire nor sell labour-power, which in turn is rare. Second, according to the authors, the combination of capital and labour is not spread evenly within a single household either. Differentiated by gender and generation, patriarchs will control the means of production, while women and children will provide unpaid labour. This analysis shows clearly that it is in the capitalist system that petty-commodity production is steadily entrenched.

Further observation by Shivji (1987:112-13) on the nature and character of small peasant production indicates that it is characterized by an extremely low level of productive forces, due to a lack of social organization of the labour process and the use of primitive techniques and technology, that is to say backwardness of the instruments of labour. Moreover, its character is highly individual, based on a household which forms both the unit of consumption as well as the supplier of labour for imperialist domination. While destroying the original division of labour, small peasant production integrated the patriarchal peasant into the new international division of labour, whereby h/she became the producer of export crops, answering to the needs of capital. Despite the low rate of surplus labour, Shivji convincingly argues and concludes that the small peasant is the main source of surplus for various exploiters and the target of a very high degree of exploitation.

Moreover, it is also asserted that in most of sub-Saharan Africa, with the exception of the territories with the most extensive (white) settlement (Kenya, former Southern Rhodesia and South Africa), 'peasant' farmers (including pastoralists) were not dispossessed but 'encouraged' by various means to enter the monetary (commodity) economy as producers of agricultural commodities and/or labour-power. In effect, the conditions of full proletarianization of the great majority of producers were not established, as Samir Amin and many others have emphasized. The means of 'encouragement' are said to include taxation, obligation to cultivate certain crops, provision of labour services or acceding to (migrant) labour contracts (Bernstein 2005:70). However, far from being 'encouragement', this was a deliberate attempt to dispossess peasant farmers by destroying the existing indigenous economy and imposing relations of exploitation through imperialist domination.

This is in line with the argument advanced by Luxemburg ([1913] 1951:368) that we must distinguish three phases: the struggle of capital against the natural economy, the struggle against the commodity economy, and the competitive struggle of capital on the international stage for the remaining conditions of accumulation. Luxemburg is of the view that the existence and development of capitalism requires an environment of non-capitalist forms of production, but not every one of these forms will serve its end. Capitalism needs non-capitalist social strata as a market for its surplus value, as a source of supply for its means of production and as a reservoir of labour power for its wage system. She states that for all these purposes, forms of production based on a natural economy are of no use to capital.

The roots of the agrarian question, as noted by Shivji (1987:111), must be traced to the superexploitation of the peasantry by imperialism in alliance with the local compradorial classes, in which the overall economy is characterized as a colonial, vertically integrated economy and the social formation as a neocolonial, semi-patriarchal one. During the colonial era, for example, the colonial state, through the mechanism of the law and the market economy, greatly increased the cash requirements of the peasantry (Tenga 1987:40). The system of imposing fixed flat rate taxes required the peasants, even in the face of declining prices, to increase production of marketable crops. Tenga states that hand in hand with the taxation system, laws were enacted that obliged the peasant to cultivate a minimum acreage of export crops, while at the same time marketing arrangements were erected through local government bodies, crop marketing boards and later the cooperatives. He demonstrates that under the Native Authority Ordinances of 1926, native authorities made by-laws to enforce agricultural cultivation and land use. This was also done under various other crop ordinances, including the Native Coffee (Control and Marketing) Ord. 1937; Plant Pest and Disease Ord. 1921 and Native Tobacco (Control and Marketing) Ord. 1940. Regulations were enacted on land use for specific crops, the breach of which was punishable by imprisonment and fines. This situation shows that the peasant was compelled to undertake economic activity favourable to the colonial economy on pain of criminal sanction.

Throughout colonial rule, there existed institutional arrangements and structures that suppressed the peasant's productive activity and perpetuated exploitation in order for him/her to produce for the colonial economy. After independence, the situation still did not favour the peasant, despite the policy of *Ujamaa*, which many scholars see as having failed to transform agriculture and the peasantry. The independent state inherited the colonial state's controls over the peasantry. In addition to the statutory controls, the post-independence state adroitly used the ruling party and its organs, as well as explicit political measures to enhance and deepen its control over the peasantry. This can be seen in the various 'rural development policies' since independence, including the decentralization of the early 1970s, the forced villagization of 1974–76 and the establishment of village governments since 1975 (Shivji 1987:123).

Commoditization and the appropriation of land in Tanzania under neoliberalism have also perpetuated the exploitation of the peasants, and have had an adverse impact on their livelihoods. An explicit surge in land-grabbing by foreign companies and 'investors' (to be explained in detail below) has not only deepened exploitation but also exposed peasants, pastoralists and local communities to various forms of dispossession and displacement, thus shaping the current agrarian question in Tanzania.

Other Approaches to the Agrarian Question in Tanzania

Since colonial times, the state has been instrumental in formulating various agrarian policies and reforms in Tanzania. These policies had different results in terms of affecting the social and economic conditions of the users of the land and in terms of the accumulation of capital by the state and the land users themselves. The latter may accumulate wealth, may remain poor or may even be pauperized because of state policies. The state itself may be successful in exploiting its land users, or it may fail to collect tax and other sources of income from them. The state formulates land laws and shapes the land tenure, which itself influences the level and kind of accumulation of capital and other types of wealth. Land tenure has a direct bearing on the agrarian question. Like other institutions (notably technology and marketing institutions) it influences accumulation and the development of farming.

Agrarian Populism and Artificial Land Shortage

Ujamaa was the populism of the first postindependence president (Julius K. Nyerere) of Tanganyika and later Tanzania. This version of populism was overwhelmingly agrarian and even anti-industrial. Peasants were moved to communal villages, and economies of scale were expected to be achieved by collectivizing labour and farms. There was a utopian belief underlying this populism, namely that a modern nation could emerge out of communal villages. Populists have traditionally opposed both feudalism and the modern commercial-ization of peasant agriculture, and accumulation of capital by peasants and the state was at its lowest when the policy was implemented over the 20 years between 1975 and 1995) (Maghimbi 1995:24; Wuyts 2008:5).

The creation of communal villages was the main agrarian movement in the history of peasant agriculture in the country. Isaiah Berlin has argued that vacillations and confusions are characteristic of mainstream populism. These were well reflected in Nyerere's populist theory of African Socialism (Berlin 1979:230-3; Maghimbi 1995:28).

Nyerere conceived an astonishingly simple scheme of how the new villages were to be organized. A new village (by then popularly called an *ujamaa* or literally a *socialist* village) was a productive association and its establishment could be initiated by any person, as long as there was democratic discussion by potential members. These members would then form a nuclear village and work on socialist principles by sharing the wealth created on the basis of their labour contribution. They would be able to save resources and invest in technology, starting with simple technology, and raise their standards of living. Initiating *ujamaa* villages would not be hard in areas with much unfarmed land. Nevertheless, Nyerere also encouraged socialism in settled areas, where peasants were supposed to engage in communal projects, such as pooling some of their land for communal production or starting projects requiring less land than crop farming, such as dairy and poultry projects (Nyerere 1967; Maghimbi 1995:28).

Much effort was put into implementing the *Ujamaa* agrarian programme after 1967, when the authorities adopted socialism as the official policy of the country. The theory of African Socialism had been published earlier in 1962 by Nyerere. However, by 1969 only 300,000 people were living in communal villages, equivalent to only 2.5 per cent of the population of an overwhelmingly agrarian country. By 1973, there were 5,628 communal (*Ujamaa*) villages in the country, with a population of 2,028,110. This was still only 15 per cent of the rural population and 12.7 per cent of the whole population (McHenry 1979:117; Maghimbi 1995:31).

In September 1973, the biennial conference of the Tanganyika African National Union (TANU, then the sole party on the mainland) resolved that living in a communal (*Ujamaa*) village was no longer voluntary. The whole of the rural population was given until the end of 1973 to live in communal villages. What followed was the uprooting of seven million people from traditional villages and their forceful resettlement in the nucleated communal villages. In heavily settled areas, new villages were administratively created by instituting every 250 households as a new village. By the end of 1976, the whole rural population of 13 million people was living in 8,320 nucleated communal villages (Coulson 1977:93; Maghimbi 1995:32).

Peasant agriculture had performed quite well during the 1950s and 1960s. This is reflected in the high growth of GDP from 1960 to 1976, 4.8 per cent per annum. This stagnated or declined from 1976 to 1995. From 1995 to 2005, the average annual growth rate picked up again and was about 5.1 per cent per annum in the latter year. The new villages were created with promises of services like water and dispensaries, but the creation of nucleated villages meant that some established farms were abandoned and this contributed to agricultural decline. Close settlement of rural households also meant the creation of land shortages even in areas where there was abundant land. This has been described as an artificial land shortage by Maghimbi (1999a:118): as the land near the village centre was all farmed, it became uneconomical for peasants to walk beyond a certain point from the village to establish new farms. Thus, in many places in the country peasants faced land shortage in the villages, while there was good unoccupied farmland only ten miles or so from the village.

Innovative peasants may move and open farms on the margins of villages in areas with much unoccupied land, such as in the regions of Morogoro, Iringa, Songea, Tabora and Lindi. However, other peasants are likely to do the same and the earlier settler has little advantage, as sooner or later he or she is ringed by other peasants and cannot expand his or her farm. This undercuts the peasants' ability to accumulate wealth by expanding acreage (Maghimbi 1999a and b). This is a little understood aspect of land tenure in peasant agriculture in Tanzania and it occurs because peasants always farm land without title deeds. It should also be mentioned that the custom of subdividing peasant farms (for the peasants' male children and occasionally daughters) each generation means that farms are very small.

There has never been land consolidation in Tanzania and land fragmentation in peasant agriculture is extreme.

In the agrarian populism of *Ujamaa*, the government was trying to increase agricultural output and reduce inequality at the same time. Some peasants had accumulated considerable wealth in the 1950s and 1960s. In places like Mbulu and Iringa these successful peasants had relatively large farms of over 130 acres (Maghimbi 1999b:81). In the late 1960s and in the 1970s, a campaign was mounted against the successful peasants, who strictly speaking were no longer peasants. They had accumulated much wealth, such as land and tractors. Some were rich peasants or *kulaks*, but some had become commercial farmers. Some of the latter lost land when it was parcelled out to poorer neighbours. They were discouraged from hiring labour by TANU political authorities. It appears the party was interested in maintaining a homogeneous African peasantry farming on the smallest scale, easy to control politically and to dominate socially. Nevertheless, this policy was not new and the restricted accumulation of wealth by peasants in the country must be viewed from a historical perspective.

The British government in Tanganyika also had a vision of a solid, homogeneous African peasantry, easily controlled and dominated. It enacted several pieces of legislation to restrict the activities of African peasants in respect of credit, trade and lease-land ownership. Lease land consisted of large surveyed farms, many of them situated on the best agricultural land. The British authorities also discouraged peasants from hiring labour. In the 1950s, some colonial officials complained that a number of wealthy natives were employing labourers to cultivate for them on Crown land. The colonial government was of the opinion that a native should only be allowed as much land as he and his family could cultivate themselves (McCarthy 1982:125; Maghimbi 1990:274-5).

From the late 1960s to the 1970s, the government encouraged accumulation at village level through the village farm. This was a large communal farm owned by members of a communal village. The idea was that economies of scale could be achieved. The communal farm led to wasteful farming and disincentivization and was quickly abandoned in favour of the block farm, which was a collection of many small peasant plots each worked individually by the owners.

In communal farming, the typical socialist problem of how to measure the individual's productivity and creativity rose. The hardest working and most creative individuals felt their labour was being averaged against that of the laziest and least creative. They felt exploited and put less effort into the communal enterprise. This did not make the lazy and less creative member work harder, because it was not easy to calculate their contribution to output and penalize the laggards (Maghimbi 1995:32).

The Tragedy of the Commons

The extreme parcelling of farmland and widespread inefficiency in the management of natural resources in and near villages in Tanzania hinders accumulation of wealth by peasants and the state. The slow growth of agriculture also means slow growth of the national economy and a deepening social crisis, as poor farming conditions increase rural-urban migration to rates that towns cannot absorb. The failure to develop clear and secure land tenure and competitive marketing institutions for peasant crops is a failure to build the necessary institutions for an agrarian revolution. The institutions of land tenure and markets are weak, considering that institutions are rules that structure human interactions and facilitate coordination among people. Many processes interact to influence the direction of institutional change, and these include the interaction between institutions and organizations, which can be viewed as the bodies created to take advantage of the opportunities determined by institutions (Platteau 2000).

The tragedy of the commons is found in land- and other resource-use in Tanzania, but this phenomenon can only be grasped if we first understand the Evolutionary Theory of Land Rights (ETLR). ETLR can also help us appreciate the point that the current peasant farming system in Tanzania and its land rights is not conducive to a green revolution and the enhancement of efficiency. This theory, and other related ones also help us to depart from the classical view of agrarian issues, which appear to be monolithic.

Currently, there is anarchy in resource-use in all areas in Tanzania where agriculture is practised in the traditional way, without title deeds from the state. This way of using land leads to parcelization and has arrested the agrarian revolution in Tanzania. A green revolution cannot occur when peasants, including pastoralists, cannot use their land as collateral to raise capital and when land keeps on being parcelled out to the children of peasants generation after generation. There is a need for land reform in Tanzania so that property rights in land can be clearly defined and institutionalized (Maghimbi 2003:255).

The basic contention of ETLR is that as land scarcity increases, people demand more secure land tenure (the outline of ETLR here is based on Platteau 1992 and 2000). This results in the emergence of private property rights in land, which then evolve towards greater measures of individualization and formalization. Deepening individualization of land tenure takes place along two main dimensions. One is the range of rights held and the other is the extent of autonomy afforded to the landholder in exercising those rights. The range of rights mentioned in ETLR is the package of rights enjoyed by the landholder, and these include rights of use and rights of transfer. In the evolution of land rights, rights over a piece of land typically begin to be asserted through the free choice of which crops to grow and of how to dispose of the harvest, and the ability to prevent others from exploiting the same piece of land by, for example, grazing livestock.

Additionally, in ETLR individualization in tenure grows through the gradual extension and increasing recognition of use rights. These rights include the right to recultivate the same plot even before the normal period of fallow has elapsed, and the right to plant trees and to bring about other improvements to the land. Further individualization takes place through the addition of transfer rights. In an ascending hierarchy of importance, the transfer rights comprise the right to:

- lend the land on traditional lines
- give the land away
- bequeath the land
- rent the land
- mortgage the land, and
- sell the land.

ETLR reveals that in the initial stages of individualization of land rights, the rights to rent out or sell land parcels are seriously restricted by the requirement that land ought to remain within the family or lineage – lineage heads must ensure this condition is duly abided by. This explains why their explicit permission is required before any sale of land can take place. However, as land becomes scarcer, that condition fades in importance. Further individualization is reflected in the autonomy of farmers regarding land use and especially their decisions to transfer land.

ETLR claims that with formalization, in the advanced stages of the individualization process, land transactions are increasingly supported by written evidence. The ultimate stage in this process is reached when land becomes extremely scarce and valuable. Then, the public sector becomes involved as there is a pressing demand for legally protected title. The maximum security of land tenure can then be achieved.

The contention in ETLR is that in most stages of the tenure transformation process, a spontaneous movement towards individualization and formalization of land rights unfolds under the combined pressure of growing land scarcity and increasing commercialization of land-based activities. In the final stage, this endogenous evolution must be aided by a public intervention designed to consolidate and legally sanction the rights that have emerged in the field.

The tragedy of the commons hinders accumulation by the more hard working and creative peasants who cannot expand their farms even in areas with some unfarmed land. Sometimes, they can expand their farms, but they cannot cultivate continuous large plots, as other peasants and land users are free to interfere in the expansion. The failure or reluctance to formalize land tenure through the massive issuance of title deeds has helped to exacerbate the tragedy of the commons.

The tragedy of the commons was best explained by Lloyd when he used the example of a pasture open to all (Lloyd 1833 cited in Hardin 1968:371). As in ETLR, Lloyd's theory is historical. The pasture used in his illustration is an arrangement that may work reasonably satisfactorily for centuries in a society at a low level of development. This is because tribal wars, poaching and disease keep the numbers of both human beings and beasts well below the carrying capacity of the land.

In Lloyd's argument, the day of reckoning finally comes when the long-sought goal of social stability becomes a reality. And then:

> At this point, the inherent logic of the commons remorselessly generates tragedy. As a rational being each herdsman seeks to maximize his gain.
>
> Explicitly or implicitly, more or less consciously, he asks: "What is the utility to me of adding one more animal to my herd?" This utility has one negative and one positive component.
>
> 1. The positive component is a function of the increment of one animal. Since the herdsman receives all the proceeds from the sale of the additional animal, the positive utility is nearly +1.
> 2. The negative component is a function of the additional overgrazing created by the one more animal. Since however, the effects of overgrazing are shared by all the herdsmen, the negative utility for any particular decision-making herdsmen is only a fraction of -1.
>
> Adding together the component partial utilities, the rational herdsman concludes that the only sensible course for him to pursue is to add another animal to his herd, and another. But this is the conclusion reached by each and every rational herdsman sharing a common. Therein lies the tragedy. Each man is locked into a system that compels him to increase his herd without limit – in a world that is limited. Prior is

the destination toward which all men rush, each pursuing his own best interest in a society that believes in freedom of the commons. Freedom in a commons brings ruin to all. (Lloyd 1833, cited in Hardin 1968:371)

The authorities in Tanzania administer land on the principle of open access. This is why not much emphasis is put on the idea of title deeds or certificates of occupancy and freehold. Anybody can invade an unoccupied piece of land, which belongs to the government and is known as general land in the 1999 land laws. Normally, the authorities will recognize the use rights of the person. However, invasion of reserved land, which also belongs to the government, is common. Even invasion of other peasants' land (for instance, when the land is under fallow or after harvest) is common. All this behaviour is a consequence of the tragedy of the commons. The person who invades a piece of land feels that if he/she does not do so another person will do so and reap all the benefit. The same is the case with the person who cuts timber in a restricted area such as a forest reserve or invades a water source. Freedom in a commons brings ruin to all and is not good for creating wealth for peasants and even for the government. The tragedy goes hand in hand with the use of land and other resources, such as pastures and trees.

Quite often, the authorities complain of pastoralists invading cropland, charcoal burners indiscriminately felling trees, peasants invading land, forest reserves being invaded, water sources being destroyed, illegal fishing, illegal mining, etc. All these are consequences of the tragedy of the commons, which goes hand in hand with the open access regime.

For those opposed to secure tenure and supporting 'traditional tenure' and other populist tenure arrangements, there is always a counter-argument. For example, it is argued that the local informal order embedded in the rural community guarantees basic land rights to all villagers, and these are sufficient to induce investment. If this argument is accepted, then it could further be argued that there is no need for the state to intervene through centralized procedures aimed at formalizing land rights (Platteau 2000:141). In real life, the local informal order and the village authority cannot guarantee secure tenure and the consequence is the many land disputes in villages, which are reported daily. Reports of disputes between crop growers and pastoralists are common even within the same village (Maghimbi 2003:257).

Open access and unregulated use of pastures and other resources in Tanzania lead to inefficient exploitation of resources. The core problem is that open access and unregulated common property do not give individuals the proper incentives to act in a socially efficient way. Such property systems as 'village land', 'common pastures' and 'general land' are likely to generate externalities. A primary function of property rights is finding incentives to achieve greater internalization of externalities (Baland and Platteau 1996:36; Maghimbi 2003:257).

Tanzania has a frontier area where land is considered ownerless. This is part of the attitude associated with the tragedy of the commons. Legally, this land belongs to the government or even to a village in those areas where large parts of village land are still unfarmed. The common reference to this land further indicates how the attitude of the commons is entrenched. This land is referred to as 'pori', which literally means 'bush' or 'nobody's land'. This type of land can be titled easily and offer security for rapid agricultural development. There is also the politically sensitive question of whether the land range should be parcelled into large blocks of private ranches for the nomadic pastoralists of Tanzania. Can parcelling lead to better resource management and higher productivity? (Maghimbi 2003:237-58).

When we observe medium-size and large-scale farmers and ranchers in Tanzania, it appears they tend to do better in income and standards of living than peasants, including nomadic pastoralists. There is still enough land in Tanzania to promote some large-scale farming and ranching without disturbing the settled areas. Agricultural development needs a judicious balance of large-scale and small-scale farming and ranching. Small scale here does not mean the current petty peasant farming, but rather medium-sized family farms of 100 acres and ranches for up to 50 well-bred cattle.

Capital accumulation in agriculture goes hand in hand with land accumulation. Supporters of private property argue that it is necessary to offer individuals sufficient motives for cultivating the ground and preventing the wasteful destruction of the products of the earth. The counter-argument is that there is injustice when there is too much concentration of land and its products in a few hands.

The middle view is to argue for regulation by, for example, placing a ceiling on land ownership. This may not be necessary, as many peasants in Tanzania prefer wage employment to farming and will abandon their land when opportunities for wage employment or more lucrative businesses (that is, other than farming) arise. This reflects the harsh conditions in agriculture and the lack of capital for investing in land. Hardin argued that an alternative to the commons need not be perfectly just to be preferable. No one has invented a better system than the institution of private property coupled with legal inheritance. Private land ownership carries some injustice, but it could be argued that some injustice is preferable to total ruin (Hardin 1967 cited in Baland and Platteau 1996:36).

There are difficult theoretical and real life problems here. Authors of the classical theory on the agrarian question, such as Kautsky, Lenin and Luxemburg, had a political agenda. Nevertheless, after the collapse of socialist agriculture and socialism, the idea of forging an alliance between at least a section of the peasantry and urban proletariats has little meaning in current local and global politics. Scholars can still support peasants by, for example, arguing for support of peasant land ownership and peasant institutions, which may enable them to counter the domination of huge global business corporations.

Forms of Accumulation and the Agrarian Question

In the attempt to reduce absolute mass poverty and improve the standards of living of its people, the Tanzanian state has tried many agrarian policies, hoping that they would help increase household-level wealth and state revenue. In the 1960s, there was much focus on cooperatives and some success was registered. However, the cooperative was abandoned in the 1970s in favour of more direct state accumulation through the parastatal crop authorities and the state farms. In the 1980s, the cooperative was reintroduced and the crop authority was sidelined in favour of liberal markets. These major policies are reviewed here in relationship to the agrarian question.

Cooperatives and Agriculture in Tanzania

There were a few peasant economic associations in Tanganyika before 1932. The most famous was the Kilimanjaro Native Planters Association (KNPA), formed in 1925 to protect and promote the interests of indigenous coffee growers in the Kilimanjaro area. The KNPA assisted in the proper control of coffee planting and in advising against pests and diseases.

It assisted peasants to sell their coffee at the highest possible price and to get supplies of chemicals and other inputs necessary for the improvement of coffee production (Kimario 1992:4).

The formation of peasant associations to promote marketing and the supply of inputs was an indication that differentiation was growing among the peasantry. There has never been a homogeneous peasantry, as Chayanov has argued. However, Chayanov was also a strong supporter of peasant cooperatives and he believed they would help the peasant economy to modernize without transforming the household basis of agriculture (Chayanov 1966 and 1991).

The Cooperative Societies Ordinance was enacted in March 1932 based on the Indian Cooperative Acts of 1904 and 1912 (Kimario 1992:5). Cooperatives started registering in January 1933 and KNPA transformed itself into the famous KNCU (Kilimanjaro Native Cooperative Union). Other cooperative societies and unions evolved from the 1930s to the 1960s and the strongholds of the movement were in Kilimanjaro (coffee), Bukoba (coffee), Tukuyu (coffee), Songea (tobacco), Matengo (coffee), Ngara (coffee), Lake Zone (Mwanza, Shinyanga, Musoma) (cotton) and Meru (coffee).

Marketing cooperatives helped many peasants to accumulate wealth and in the areas where the movement was strong there were many rich peasants or *kulaks*. One cooperative (the TFA or Tanganyika Farmers Association) was constituted by commercial farmers. Some of its members became very successful farmers and owned large commercial farms, especially in Arusha region. Cooperatives help farmers to accumulate because they increase their share of the trade profit.

It was in Tanganyika that the largest cooperative movement in the whole of Africa developed, the Victoria Federation of Cooperative Unions Limited (VFCU). By 1968, the cooperative movement on the mainland was handling £ 27.5 million worth, or 45 per cent, of the country's annual exports. At the time, this share was second only to Israel and Denmark (University Press 1968:176).

Cooperatives channelled loans to individual members by acting as guarantors of loans. The Cooperative Bank of Tanganyika was founded in 1962 and changed its name to the National Cooperative Bank (NCB) in 1964. The shareholders were cooperative unions. By 1967, the bank had accumulated Tshs 1.8 million as general reserves and Tshs 1.1 million as statutory reserves. It had appropriated Tshs 250,000 for dividends, which was 7.3 per cent of its paid-up share capital. The bank provided overdrafts to cooperatives to finance the purchase of export and food crops from crop growers who were cooperative members and non-members. By 1970, the NCB had share capital of Tshs 4.5 million and made a profit of Tshs 5 million (Kimario 1992:24).

The NCB operated side by side with the National Development Credit Agency (NDCA). These two institutions operated under one parent body, the National Cooperative and Development Bank, established in 1964. The NDCA was used to grant credit to peasants.

Funds were made available from the International Development Agency (IDA) and other sources. The NDCA was able to reach about 100,000 peasants annually. Considerable sums of money were injected into the agricultural sector through the NDCA, as the table below indicates.

Agricultural Credit provided by the NDCA to Cooperatives in 1962-66

Year	No. of Cooperatives Unions	Credit to Cooperatives (Tshs)	Credit to Cooperatives and Non-cooperative members (Tshs)
1962	7	392,000.00	8,410,000.00
1963	33	1,387,000.00	7,082,000.00
1964	20	6,101,000.00	8,024,000.00
1965	45	16,207,000.00	20,013,000.00
1966	26	15,066,000.00	16,052,000.00

Source: Kimario 1992:28

It is clear that cooperatives were accumulating large capital before they were abolished in 1976. Some cooperatives gave scholarships to members' children to study abroad. The union in Kilimanjaro (KNCU) and the union in Bukoba (BNCU) each built a secondary school. KNCU even built its own business college in the mid-1950s and its own hotel. Until recently, the tallest building in Dar es Salaam was owned by the Cooperative Union of Tanzania (CUT). The table below gives an indication of the wealth created by cooperatives.

Development of Cooperatives, 1960-67

Year	No. of Registered Cooperatives	No. of members	Share capital (Tshs)	Reserves and surpluses
1960	691	236,211	4,983,000.00	60,396,220.00
1962	974	330,644	9,140,720.00	54,350,080.00
1964	1,518	607,655	11,250,620.00	97,356,920.00
1966	1,616	NA	NA	NA
1967	1,649	NA	NA	NA

Source: Kimario 1992:28

There appears to have been a contradiction between those who controlled the cooperatives (rich peasants who were the nascent agrarian bourgeoisie) and the rising bureaucracy that controlled the state. This contradiction determined the future of agricultural development in the country. Cooperatives were bringing much revenue to the government through export taxes and local government taxes. However, the class contradictions between a rising agrarian bourgeoisie and a parasitic bureaucracy led to sharp changes in policy. The state bureaucracy sought an independent source of accumulation through state or parastatal companies, which could be directly controlled by the state, unlike cooperatives, which were democratic and controlled by the rising agrarian bourgeoisie.

The NCB was abolished in 1971 following the creation of a monolithic state bank (the NBC or National Bank of Commerce) and the nationalization of foreign banks. The NDCA had been dissolved earlier, in 1970. We earlier saw that the NDCA was able to reach 100,000 peasants annually and the number was rising. The abolition of the NCB and the NDCA elicited strong opposition from cooperative members (Kimario 1992:24-5). However, cooperatives were abolished in 1976 and their crop marketing functions were allocated to parastatal crop authorities. The state's policy on agriculture also shifted from supporting peasants to supporting state farms, which, together with the parastatal crop authorities, became the focus of accumulation in agriculture by the state. It must also be mentioned that since the abolition of the NDCA and NCB the provision of credit to peasants has been a major problem. This has not helped the agrarian sector in developing and the shortage of capital to peasant farms remains one of the major hindrances to an agrarian revolution in Tanzania.

Parastatal Crop Authorities and State Farms

One parastatal crop authority was created for each major crop (cotton, coffee, sisal, cashew nuts, tea and pyrethrum). Another crop parastatal (the NMC or National Milling Corporation) was created to buy grain from peasants to sell in towns and to export. Yet another (GAPEX or General Agricultural Export Company) was created to buy and export non-traditional crops like simsim, sunflower and cardamom.

The parastatal crop companies had the monopoly of buying crops directly from peasants. This was a strategy for the state to accumulate by using government agencies. The strategy extended to other sectors, and parastatals were created to run virtually all sectors of the economy. In the 1970s and 1980s, there were 400 parastatals directly under the government.

Crop authorities made huge losses and became heavily dependent on handouts from the treasury. It is argued that they contributed a great deal to the economic decline of the country (World Bank 1983:76-7). They failed to provide price incentives to peasants; they were highly bureaucratic; and sometimes they failed to collect crops which were already in village stores. They borrowed crops from the peasants and they failed to supply the inputs the cooperatives had supplied in the past.

The idea of accumulating through parastatal companies extended to direct farming and not only marketing organizations, such as crop authorities. In the first five year development plan of the country (1964-69), agriculture was allocated 15 per cent of the investment. Most of this money (70 per cent) went to support settlement schemes which covered only a few thousand peasants. In the second five year plan (1969-74) more than 15 per cent of estimated development expenditure was set aside for agriculture, but state farms and not peasants were favoured in the spending of this money. During the plan period, one agricultural parastatal that ran state farms (NAFCO – National Agricultural and Food Corporation) received a larger investment budget than all communal (*Ujamaa*) villages put together. More than 80 per cent of the total ministerial and parastatal development budget on direct agricultural production in the plan period went to agricultural parastatals running large-scale mechanized farms. This pattern of spending continued up to at least 1990 (Freyhold 1979:92-3; Maghimbi 1990:225).

The state farms were very inefficient and overcapitalized. Favouring these farms and the crop authorities meant squeezing the peasants. In 1974, the third five year plan could not be launched. Agricultural production by peasants had represented the greater proportion of the country's output, and now peasant production was staggering, stagnating or declining for some crops. Cotton production dropped from 65,500 tonnes in 1971-72 to 44,500 in 1981-85; cashew nuts from 121,500 to 43,200 and sisal from 181,100 to 72,000 (Iane 1984:42). The country also experienced large imports of food for the first time in 1971-72 (92,000 tons of maize), while the following year some 53,000 tonnes of maize were exported. However, imports reached 317,000 tons in 1974-75 and 42,000 tons in 1975-76 (Loftchie 1978:454).

The squeeze on the peasantry became worse, not only because most of the government's investment in agriculture was going to state farms and crop authorities, but also because peasants were not able to accumulate because of the very low producer prices offered by the parastatal crop authorities. The marketing approach of the monopolistic crop authorities was that the prices paid to peasants were calculated as a residue. The residue price for the peasant was reached after the crop authority deducted all its other costs from the estimated gross sales at exportation (Gibbon and Neocosmos 1985:201).

Gibbon and Neocosmos argue that the parastatal crop authorities' marketing style shifted from giving weight to the crop growers to calculating who took what from the marketing margin. This style lent itself to the acceptance of uncritical marketing-cost projections. The parastatal crop authority was able to systematically cheat the peasant out of the revenue realized from cash crops. In social analysis, this 'cheating' was viewed to be a consequence of the petty-bourgeois form of organization of the state generally, and its economic enterprises in particular. This form of organization allowed mismanagement and accumulation of wealth by individual managers of the parastatal organizations (Gibbon and Neocosmos 1985:201).

As many peasants became poorer due to low returns from their crops, some peasants indulged in strategies of petty wealth creation by bypassing the state marketing monopolies. They attempted to sell their crops in unofficial markets, including markets across borders. Other peasants replaced crops handled by crop authorities with crops with no marketing restrictions: for example, some peasants in Kilimanjaro area famously replaced coffee with tomatoes and dairy cows. In the Coast region, some peasants neglected their cashew farms and opted for charcoal burning (Maghimbi 1990:279).

The state farms did not make any profit and the crop authorities were inefficient and corrupt. They were also too big, since one crop authority served the whole country. The Tanzania Cashew Nut Authority (TCA), like other crop authorities, failed to provide market incentives to peasants. This, combined with the disruptions caused by villagization in 1973-76, led to a near collapse of the cashew industry and increased the pauperization of peasants in Mtwara, Lindi and Coast regions. Some villagers had abandoned their cashew farms when they were moved to the new nucleated villages. Such people were unlikely to tend their cashew trees on their old farms unless prices were attractive. They were also reluctant to plant new trees, because they feared another government policy that might require them to move again. They also had less land, on account of the policy of concentrating people in nucleated villages, which created the artificial land shortage mentioned earlier. Production of cashews had increased from 40,000 tons in 1960-61 to 118,000 tonnes in 1967-68 and

145,000 tonnes in 1973-74. It then declined to 57,000 tonnes in 1978-79 and 17,000 tons in 1986-87 (Maghimbi 1990:270-1).

Gibbon and Neocosmos point to the petty-bourgeois class character of the Tanzanian state as the cause of the systematic failure to develop, implement and sustain consistent policies and the means to monitor them. They argue that the petty-bourgeois state meant different things at different times: modernist and nativist, bureaucratic and popular, reactionary and progressive, statist and anarchist, consumerist and ascetic, cynical and idealist, aggressive and timid and grandiose and apathetic. Its tendency was to seek quick victory by resorting to populist policies like African Socialism and by bombarding its population with ever-new commands, institutions and campaigns (Gibbon and Neocosmos 1985:192-3).

Gibbon and Neocosmos have advanced our understanding of the agrarian question in Tanzania. The argument they put forward is that many of the (failed) agrarian policies and practices in Tanzania lie in the petty-bourgeois class character of the postcolonial state. This is a state that displays the internal contradictions of petty-bourgeois practices.

It was very hard for the class of small and large agrarian entrepreneurs to develop during the 1970s and 1980s, because these farmers had depended on the abolished cooperatives to accumulate. Moreover, parastatal companies (crop authorities, state farms, regional trading companies) monopolized the handling of traditional crops and the wholesale and sometimes even retail trade. Such arrangements discouraged the growth of agrarian classes and the creation of wealth and jobs in rural areas. Because Tanzania's economy depended so much on export crops, even the urban economy declined. Changes were needed in agricultural policy if agricultural stagnation and decline were to be reversed.

Agriculture and Economic Liberalization Policies

The poor performance of the agricultural sector in the 1970s and 1980s was accompanied by severe food insecurity, decreased export earnings and general economic stagnation. This hindered the accumulation of wealth even by that small class that had formulated the state capitalism policies which resulted in state-sponsored monopolistic companies in the form of crop authorities, state farms, regional trading companies, etc. These policies were discouraging the growth of rural labour markets (Mduma 2006:7).

The policies that succeeded the era of state capitalism and continue up to the present have been described as liberalization policies and began in 1986 with the programmes of structural adjustment. It is well known that the World Bank had a hand in these policies (Mduma 2006:7-8). Under the new policy, peasant cooperatives were allowed to operate but crop merchants were also free to buy crops from peasants. Export tax was abolished for all items and in 1993 export licensing was abolished on everything except natural resources. There was a temporary reintroduction of export taxes on traditional exports in 1996-97 and in 2002. In 2003, zero-rated Value Added Tax (VAT) was imposed on all agricultural imports and outputs (Mduma 2006:8-9).

Now crop merchants cannot buy crops directly from peasants, but this regulation applies only to traditional crops like coffee, cashew nuts and cotton. Subsidies on agricultural inputs were first abolished under the structural adjustment policies but recently were reintroduced. However, it has been observed that Tanzania's agriculture is still a household farm-based sector, with about 70 per cent of the crop area cultivated by hand hoe, 20 per cent by ox plough and only 10 per cent by tractor. Agricultural production is mainly dependent on rain-fed cultivation. Small farms dominate and peasants cultivate household farms that are on average as small as 0.9 hectares and rarely exceed 3 hectares. Food crops are the same as in the past, namely rice, bananas, maize, cassava, beans, millet, sorghum, sweet potatoes and Irish potatoes. Cash crops are still traditional, namely cotton, coffee, tobacco, cashew nuts, tea, cloves, sugar, pyrethrum, coconuts, cardamom and groundnuts (Mduma 2006:11). Tomatoes, onions, oranges, pineapples, carrots, water melons, cucumbers, green peppers and cabbages are also commonly grown as cash crops. Currently, cooperatives are in operation but it is hard to showcase many peasants moving out of absolute poverty. Accumulation at all levels is low because of poor technology, as is labour productivity (Mduma 2006:11).

According to Mduma (2006:9), the structure of Tanzanian agriculture and of the economy as a whole has remained virtually unchanged despite liberalization initiatives. This implies that accumulation is slow at both the level of the state and the household. The major components of the agricultural sector are food crops, which account for 55 per cent of agricultural GDP, and livestock, which accounts for 30 per cent. Traditional export crops account for 8 per cent, while fishing, forestry and hunting account for the remaining 7 per cent (Mduma 2006:8-9).

Some peasants have taken advantage of liberalized policies to increase their incomes. According to the director and registrar of cooperatives, in 2009 there were 7,868 primary cooperatives in the country. From 2004, some primary cooperatives decided to bypass their cooperative union in selling coffee. For example, cooperatives in Rombo district in Kilimanjaro region bypassed the KNCU and were able to get Tshs 1,286.02 per kg of coffee. This was a significant improvement on the Tshs 600 offered to the cooperatives through traditional market channels.

The problem of scale is still a major obstacle in the way of increased wealth creation. Given the scale of production for most peasants in Tanzania, even if higher prices were offered, they would remain poor. This is why the idea of land consolidation through land reform and allowing a land market to develop is important. An average peasant coffee farm was only 0.6 hectares in 1975. The average in the Kilimanjaro area was 0.73 acres in 1930 and would be much smaller now because there has never been land consolidation in the country (Maghimbi 2007:75-7). Even with intensification, it is not easy to increase output on such small plots. The population increase is high but the Boserupian theory of increasing density and increasing productivity does not seem to operate in Tanzania. The population of Kilimanjaro region rose from 662,722 in 1967 to 1,381,149 in 2002 and in the same period the density increased from 49 to 104 per square kilometre (URT 2003:2-7; Maghimbi 2007:77).

Liberalization has not addressed the problem of parcelling land into millions of tiny farms. However, the 1999 Land Laws contain important provisions with the potential to increase the security of women's rights to land, such as joint titling, consent clauses and the stipulation of equality between men and women in land matters. Most peasants' land is still held without any title deed or certificate of occupancy and few women own land. Scholars still question whether the provisions for increasing the security of women's rights to land can actually be implemented. The law recognizes customary land rights, which overwhelmingly favour men. It also recognizes individualized land tenure and a peasant in a village can register his or her land and get a title deed from the village. Ikdahl takes the view that neither laws based on inducing rapid individualization nor those building on idealized notions of static and communal 'customary land tenure' can guarantee equal benefits for men and women. For Ikdahl, a basic premise is that women are given equal rights in law. She argues that the state must perform a balancing act, for which the human rights framework provides guidelines (Ikdahl 2008:55-6).

Departing from small farms seems not to be on the agenda of policymakers. There is the example of the currently proposed paddy project in the Rufiji River Basin. It was reported (*The Guardian*, 20 November 2009) that the governments of Tanzania and South Korea will support a project to create 50,000 modern farmers. The Sokoine University of Agriculture is involved in a training centre set up in the Basin to train farmers. The report indicates that the project aims at moving farmers from small-scale to large-scale farming so they can double their income through the production of paddy and other crops using modern technology, including tractors. However, only 100,000 acres of land have been allocated for the project, so that this project could still end up reproducing farming on the smallest scale.

The Green Revolution/Kilimo Kwanza

Historically, land reform has been critical to agrarian reform and agricultural development (Moyo 2004b). In Tanzania, there has been a failure to make the necessary institutional, technical and structural shifts.

One student of the green revolution in India in the 1970s argues that its success lay in the institutional and structural shifts, the strengthening of marketing cooperatives, the growth and consolidation of the rich peasantry and credit flows to these peasants. Indian rural society had undergone institutional and structural shifts in the previous two decades. The most important of these mentioned by scholars is land reform, which included consolidation and security of land ownership. These changes created the prerequisites for part of the Indian peasantry to stage a technological breakthrough (Maghimbi 1999b:83).

The 1999 Land Laws provide for certificates of occupancy. Indeed, this provision has been there since German days in some form or other. The only major change in law was the abolition of freehold after independence. The problem is that since colonial days, the approach to land in Tanganyika and later Tanzania has focused on land law and not on the structural constraints to change of an agrarian/green revolution type. It appears that agricultural development is very difficult to achieve under the current land tenure on peasant farms. A few medium- and large-scale farmers have been very successful, one reason for which is that they have titled their land and have security of tenure and access to credit.

Agrarian reform is expensive to implement. There are millions of tiny peasant farms that are not surveyed, like the tiny *microfincas* in Latin America. They are so small a surveyor would need a microscope to locate them on a cadastral map of any scale. Land consolidation is necessary under such circumstances. Because land reform is so costly, the other solution is to encourage land sales so that consolidation takes place spontaneously. Land reform can be implemented through a law that restricts the minimum acreage for farms. This will stop the parcelling of farmland into uneconomical plots.

There is still much good agricultural land in Tanzania that is unfarmed. It would appear that land reform is not so hard to implement. However, land reform is a political process, which will lead to the growth and consolidation of a class of rich peasants and other commercial farmers. Political will is thus required before land reform can be implemented. Land reform can also target a few districts with high potential, and continue gradually. Because of the current insecure tenure, there is much waste in the use of land and other resources like water and trees.

The Land (Amendment) Act 2004 and the Mortgage Financing (Special Provisions) Act 2008 are amendments to the Land Act 1999 (Cap 113), aimed at making it easier to use land to raise capital. These laws also aim at making the mortgaging of land more convenient and protecting both the mortgagee and mortgagor. These amendments for the first time allow the sale of bare land, although in reality such sales are common. When we consider peasant land, it is still not easy for most peasants to raise capital. For the time being, the focus of policy should be on new agricultural land, where surveying and titling of peasant family farms of about 100 acres per family should be made compulsory. These farms will help to create millions of rural jobs. Under the current tenure, land is wastefully cultivated and quite often abandoned by peasants when they get wage employment or other more rewarding economic activities, like retail opportunities or jobs in town.

Technological change is slow in Tanzania. The current government programme for agricultural development, *Kilimo Kwanza*, (Agriculture First) is too recent to be evaluated, having been launched in 2009. Although technology and land are mentioned in the programme, the former requires clearer exposition. There are about four million peasant families in Tanzania and only about 15 per cent of the 883,989 sq.km. of total land area is cultivated. The average family farm measures only two acres and 93 per cent of all peasant families cultivate less than five acres. There are only 6,000 working tractors (a drop from 20,000 in 1970), and factories to process crops and meat are lacking, although the country has about 18 million cattle and 15 million goats (Maghimbi 1999b). It is not easy to transform this structure and one planning strategy would be to concentrate on new agricultural land where the proposed medium-sized family farms can be easily surveyed and titled.

Many issues in the development of the sector revolve around the *Kilimo Kwanza* requirements. A key area is investment in the rapid modernization and professionalization of the agricultural sector, with a strong focus on maximum productivity and output growth. The implication is that the agricultural sector really has to orient itself towards the market. This cannot be done with traditional cash crops such as coffee, cotton, sisal and tea, but requires new non-traditional crops. In this programme, government strongly encourages the initiative of the private sector. It is obvious that smallholder farmers will be pushed off the land and the danger is that, if care is not taken, mounting tension over land is likely to arise in many places. Tanzanian peasants lack political power, and risk being marginalized as large-scale global agribusinesses increase their operations in the country.

Kilimo Kwanza aims at modernizing small-, medium- and large-scale farmers. It is a typical blanket policy, but not everybody can become a modern farmer and it is not desirable that all who call themselves farmers should become professional farmers. It is necessary to identify and target the more serious farmers, otherwise resources may be spread too thinly. One of the authors of this paper saw shifting farmers, also called tractor landlords, in Kiteto district in 2005. These have invaded large areas of the district, clearing land in villages and government land ('general land'), farming only one maize crop and then moving on. They add no inputs to the land, but make huge profits because they cultivate virgin land. They can make a profit of about $ 10,000 in one maize season for a $ 2,000 investment in a farm of about 80 acres. The tractor landlords (also called 'Wabena' in Kiteto) currently abuse the land, but they could be identified as entrepreneurs to be given certificates of occupancy on large farms and encouraged to settle on their farms and practise permanent agriculture. Their shifting practices can be explained by the presence of an open access regime and the absence of well-defined property rights. Lack of strong institutions to govern farming behaviour is killing agricultural development in Tanzania. Land tenure is a fundamental institution, whose operation can determine the balance of class forces and the outcome of social conflicts in a peasant-dominated society such as Tanzania (Platteau 2000). Land tenure exerts a significant influence on agricultural growth. Too much time is wasted in walking to the farm, because a peasant family will comprise three and even up to ten small plots, which look like gardens. Land reform can aim at consolidation, which can also be stimulated by a well-developed and regulated land market.

Accumulation by Dispossession and the Agrarian Question

Tanzania is not alone in witnessing the intensification of what geographer David Harvey (2003) calls accumulation by dispossession. This is an often violent and predatory process in which so-called 'investors', backed by capitalist states, usually expand their influence and role by dispossessing indigenous peoples, peasants and pastoralists of their land and livelihoods. These people are forced to turn to the labour market in order to survive, creating a pool of cheap labour for corporate enterprises to exploit, while the 'investors' themselves gain unhindered access to the resources on the now unoccupied land – agricultural land, mining land or hunting land.

Harvey wanted to explain the processes of accumulation in the era of neoliberalism. According to Shivji (2009a:34), Harvey combines Lenin's thesis of over-accumulation and Luxemburg's proposition on continued processes of primitive accumulation[6] in the encounter between capitalist and non-capitalist modes, to deepen our understanding of the current stage of capitalist imperialism. The argument is that the two forms of capitalist accumulation, that is accumulation through expanded reproduction and accumulation through primitive means, continue to operate throughout the history of capitalist accumulation on a world scale. Here, Shivji states, Harvey examines how the "'organic relation' between expanded reproduction on the one hand and the often violent processes of dispossession on the other have shaped the historical geography of capitalism" (Shivji 2009a:33-4).

Harvey reminds us that primitive accumulation remains one of capitalism's persistent tactics:

> ... a closer look at Marx's description of primitive accumulation reveals a wide range of processes. These include the commodification and privatisation of land and the forceful expulsion of peasant populations; conversion of various forms of property rights (common, collective, state, etc.) into exclusive private property rights; suppression of rights to the commons; commodification of labor power and the suppression of alternative (indigenous) forms of production and consumption; colonial, neo-colonial and imperial processes of appropriation of assets (including natural resources); monetisation of exchange and taxation (particularly of land); slave trade; and usury, the national debt and ultimately the credit system as radical means of primitive accumulation. (2003:145).

---

6. Shivji (2009a:26) specifies that primitive accumulation is the original process by which the conditions of the process of capitalist accumulation are created. Capitalist production assumes a set of people with capital or money, on the one hand, and another set of people who have nothing else by which to subsist and reproduce themselves except their own human energy or muscle power, on the other. Nature did not produce property-less labourers on one side and owners of property on the other: they had to be created. Producers had to be expropriated from their means of production and this process of separation of producers from their means of production is the historical process of primitive accumulation.

For Harvey (2003:145-6), all features of primitive accumulation that Marx mentions have remained powerfully present in capitalism's historical geography until now, and displacement of peasant populations and the formation of a landless proletariat has accelerated in countries such as Mexico and India in the last three decades. Many formerly common property resources, such as water, have been privatized (often at World Bank insistence) and brought within the capitalist logic of accumulation; alternative (indigenous and even, in the case of the US, petty commodity) forms of production and consumption have been suppressed. Nationalized industries have been privatized and family farming has been taken over by agribusiness.

What Marx uncovered and wrote about the violent separation of the labouring poor from their means of production and the accumulation through loot and plunder that went along with it – with subsequent accounts added to it – is now paralleled by the violence meted out to peasants and pastoralists. Primitive accumulation can now be seen as a violent, prehistoric event in the emergence of capitalist nature, a violent disruption and rearticulating of nature, including human nature as incorporated into capital. As already noted, this state of affairs prevails in Tanzania (as selected cases will demonstrate), and greatly intensifies the agrarian question. Peasants are active agents and the presence of primitive accumulation does not mean that there is a law of nature that will always exclude peasants themselves from accumulating land and other wealth. A strong regime supporting local peasant capitalism has not yet emerged. The petty-bourgeois class character of the state is thus likely to have a bearing on what occurs to the Tanzanian peasantry. From the earlier remarks of Gibbon and Neocosmos we can conclude that it is very hard to predict the policies of such a state and their outcome.

The state in Tanzania is central to primitive accumulation. As Moyo notes (2007:7), large tracts of land in many African countries are controlled by the state through various property relations. State agencies hold land directly and indirectly; the state has powers over local authorities that control land under customary tenure; and, through its regulatory instruments, the state wields powers over statutory lands, particularly leasehold lands and land markets. State power and political hegemony over national territory is expressed specifically through powers over the allocation of land and related resources, the regulation of land tenure and land use, and through state structures responsible for the resolution of disputes that arise from competing claims to land. Such control is accompanied by extensive state influence over the allocation and use of water and natural resources, and, through this and other economic policies, the state directs financial resources and incentives that influence patterns of land utilization. Moyo clearly argues that the African state, situated within the context of neocolonial class formation processes and extroverted economic structures, is itself shaped by differentiated internal social forces that define political power and accumulation, but these remain subordinated to external capital and markets. He further argues that the state is still central to 'primitive accumulation' in general and access to major national socioeconomic resources in particular, given the absence of a mature indigenous bourgeoisie. Access to political office can be critical to the direction of accumulation. Weak neocolonial African states, whether these were formerly settler colonies or not, retain different degrees of 'customary' regimes of authority, including some forms akin to remnants of semi-feudal regimes, such as those found in Morocco and northern Nigeria. These play a critical role, together with central and local governments, in the control and allocation of land.

As already noted, Tanzania has witnessed various initiatives to dispossess peasants and pastoralists of natural resources and land, which is an important component of the agrarian question. Sulle and Nelson (2009:3) for example, have found that over four million hectares of land have been requested for bio-fuel investments, particularly jatropha, sugar cane and oil palm, although only 640,000 ha have so far been allocated and formal rights of occupancy have been granted to only about 100,000 ha of these. Some companies are proposing bio-fuel projects involving initial investments of up to US$ 1 billion, or several billion US$ over the next 10-20 years. Both the Tanzanian and foreign governments have been promoting this surge in bio-fuel investments. Sulle and Nelson caution that growing commercial pressures on rural lands, such as agrifood, tourism, and now bio-fuels, may create economic interests for government agencies to allocate more lands to large-scale investments. More discussion of this state of affairs is provided in the subsequent section.

Balancing the national interest of promoting investment with the private interests of government policymakers who may themselves be involved in such businesses, and the land access interests of smallholder farmers and pastoralists has been one of the most contentious aspects of land tenure debates in Tanzania over the past 20 years. This confirms how the state has been central to primitive accumulation as a particular historical event or process, in which the preconditions of capitalism were brought together by a process of accumulation by dispossession, which could then continue side by side with the 'mainstream' process of accumulation. As noted by Harvey (2005), accumulation by dispossession is a politically driven process that occurs simultaneously with capital accumulation. It works in a variety of ways, from the subtle commodification of once communal property to outright theft. It is essentially contingent and ad hoc, whereas capital accumulation is systematic.

Sometimes, the land targeted for investment is normally used for the livelihood-based activities on which local communities heavily depend. Dispossessing local communities by any means, including the transfer of land from village to general land, has the adverse effect of extinguishing customary rights over the same and permanently restricting engagement in livelihood-activities in the village realm. What is expected to result from these is the intensification of accumulation by dispossession and the perpetuation of the agrarian question.

Agro-fuels, Large-Scale Food Production and New Land Grabs

The continuously rising price of petroleum over the past decade and the progressive depletion of fossil fuel reserves have triggered several global innovations in search of sustainable alternative energy sources such as bio-fuels. This has been further accelerated by the ever-increasing demand for fossil fuel in the world, and in the fast growing economies of China and India. Some countries, namely Brazil, the US and those of Western Europe, are in the forefront of the development of these alternative energy sources, while others, including Tanzania, are newcomers. They need to learn carefully from the experiences of global leaders in the bio-fuel industry to avoid mistakes and optimize benefits.

Bio-fuels remain highly contentious in Tanzania. There has been a huge wave of foreign investors into the country since 2005. Currently, a large area of land is being set aside for investors in bio-fuel production. If not properly monitored and regulated, these activities could lead to a great many rural populations being displaced, with potentially serious effects on the country's long-term political stability. Some of the major land conflicts relating to bio-fuels have arisen from the controversial labelling of land as barren, idle, degraded and marginal. These labels have been called into question, with some stakeholders claiming the land is not available when traditional pastoralists who roam across large areas of the country are taken into account. Most of the land has been defined as general land since most villages have not registered the land as village land. However, nearby villagers do have customary rights stemming from longstanding occupation or use of the land. The key pieces of legislation governing land holding and administration are the Land Act (1999) and the Village Land Act (1999). While section 8 of the latter act provides for the powers of managing village land to be vested in the village council, management of other land use categories is largely vested in the Commissioner for Lands (section 10 of the Land Act). The more the villages demarcate their land, the more land administration shifts towards the villages. The fact that in some instances other legislation has been employed to facilitate land acquisition and use, especially for investment projects, creates the potential for conflict.

An analysis of district land uses reveals that even those lands where bio-fuel production has been indicated as potentially feasible are currently accommodating or designated for other uses, such as settlements, grazing, mining and cultivation (Mwamila et al. 2009). The implication is that introducing new uses in such areas will create competition that, if not well managed, may culminate in conflict. There is therefore an urgent need to prepare land use plans at village, district, regional and zonal levels, taking into account present and future land uses and the potential for large-scale bio-fuel production areas.

Land Tenure, Land Reform and Peasant Agriculture

As noted above, current land tenure in Tanzania is guided by the 1999 Land Act and the 1999 Village Land Act. All land in Tanzania is public land vested in the president as trustee on behalf of all citizens. These acts give much power to the president in land matters. The government has authority to offer title deeds of 33, 66 or 99 years for farming or other purposes. Customary rights of occupancy are recognized by these laws and a village council may offer a certificate of customary right of occupancy. In reality, very few peasants have registered their land. They farm their land as inherited farms from their parents. Quite often, peasants will also clear new land for farms and subject it to the same tenure as the land they inherited from their parents.

Most peasants are not aware of the provisions in the law that enable them to register their land and get title deeds. Actually, the law does not forbid peasants from applying for certificates of occupancy under the 1999 Land Act, which in cases of legal dispute takes precedence over the Village Land Act. It is not clear why the country has two land laws, but the logic appears to derive from colonial dualism, where a distinction was (and is) made between the modern (land held under the 1999 Land Act) and the traditional (land held under the 1999 Village Land Act). Traditional land tenure has sat well with the philosophy of the country's rulers since the days of colonialism. Both the 1923 Land Ordinance (Cap 113) and the 1999 Village Land Act recognize traditional land tenure. Strictly speaking, both colonial and postcolonial tenure is not traditional in the classical sense. Land in precolonial Tanzania was held on four very well articulated tenure arrangements, and none of them fits with colonial and postcolonial tenure in peasant agriculture.

The first type of precolonial land tenure was clan- or lineage-type land allocation and control, under which there was also the family type of land ownership and control. The second type was the centralized and hierarchical chiefly control of land allocation. The third was the quasi-feudal type of tenure where landlord clans or lineages controlled land in a manner nearing land ownership under medieval feudalism in Europe. The fourth was the slave plantations found mostly in Zanzibar and in pockets on the mainland. One author from the end of the 19th century, for example, reported seeing an Arab coconut plantation in Tabora, which was run with slave labour (Maghimbi 1990:16-17; Calvert 1917:72).

None of these tenure systems matches the currently most popular form of tenure, which involves most farmers (peasants) holding small plots of land in villages created in the late 1960s and early 1970s under the policy of socialism. These villages cannot be described as traditional, because chiefs and other traditional authorities were abolished immediately after independence in 1962. There is extreme parcelling of peasant farmland, and this was not the case in the four tenure systems mentioned above. Even so, the current tenure in peasant agriculture is still referred to as customary or traditional. Nevertheless, it is important to make the distinction so that historical reality is not distorted.

It can be argued that one of the fundamental causes of poverty and lack of capital accumulation among peasants in Tanzania is the current land tenure, which encourages small, uneconomical family farms, which cannot be used to raise capital because peasants lack title deeds. Their tiny plots of land do not qualify as collateral. Worse still, when peasants sell their land they cannot raise much capital, since the sale value of the land does not carry a collateral premium (Platteau 1992:91-4). Peasant agriculture faces two important processes that hinder accumulation at family level. These are the presence of an artificial land shortage and the operation of the law of the tragedy of the commons, as discussed in previous sections.

The De Soto Intervention

One of the most famous issues in the ongoing land reforms is the concept of promoting land as collateral. When President Mkapa was elected to office in 1995, one of his promises was to undertake major land reforms with the object of making land an asset. Promoting the use of land as collateral has been identified as one of the strategies in Tanzania's National Programme for Economic Growth and Eradication of Poverty. This idea seems to have been borrowed from Hernando De Soto's, *The Mystery of Capital.* In this famous book, which now serves as the country's Economic Manifesto, De Soto asks why capitalism triumphs in the West and fails everywhere else?

In connection with the above developments, the government moved to establish a programme on poverty and business formalization,[7] which is administered by the office of the president. The main objective of the programme is to:

> ... facilitate the transformation of properties and business in the informal sector into formal, legally held and operated entities within the emerging and growing modern and formal economy in the country. It especially targets individuals and groups in the formal sector who for a variety of reasons are unable or unwilling to join the mainstream of the current setting of the country.

These amendments have signalled a revolution in the existing land tenure framework. They

---

7. It is popularly known in Kiswahili as *Mpango wa Kurasimisha Rasilimali na Biashara za Wanyonge Tanzania* (MKURA-BITA) and in English as the *Programme to Formalize the Property and Business of the Poor in Tanzania.*

have been justified as being in the interest of Tanzanians. The reason given by the then Ministry of Lands and Human Settlements for the amendments was the facilitation of a market in land so that citizens were free to sell land they cannot develop to those with the requisite capacities (Kamata 2003; Shivji 2003). The money thus acquired could be used to invest in other areas in which the sellers of the land have a comparative advantage. The amendments have introduced one major change to the land tenure system in respect of bare land. It is now officially permissible to sell bare land, a hitherto unknown practice in the philosophy of land tenure in the country. The previous arrangements for land markets did not allow the sale of bare land, because the value of land was thought to lie in the improvements made to it as opposed to the natural soil itself.

The titling of customary rights and interests in land is akin to the granted right of occupancy. In fact, the only difference between the two is that customary titles can only be given in village lands while granted rights of occupancy can be given for all categories of land. The individualization, titling and registration (ITR) of land has the advantage of making ownership easier to prove and hence seemingly strengthens security of tenure. It also makes it easier for land to be used in borrowing. However, it needs to be noted that making ownership easy to prove through titles also means it would be easy to change: hence, security of tenure could also be compromised. It can also encourage individualism and hence lead to conflicts in land use among people who have a tradition of sharing resources, such as pastoralists.

The programme allegedly aims to empower the poor to capitalize their assets and hence alleviate poverty. Formalization of property rights has the advantage of making them useful in securing the loans necessary for generating capital. But the advantage ends if one defaults on loan repayments, with the consequent prospect of merciless and irrevocable foreclosure. So, formalization of property can also, as it has in many other countries, lead to formalization of dispossession and its concomitant destitution and marginalization (Olenasha 2003). For land and other property to be used as collateral, it must be held 'legally' – privatized, registered and titled. According to the De Soto logic, land and other property owned and held under customary law do not belong to anyone and as such are not property in the strict sense. Therefore, they cannot be used productively to generate further capital. One important factor was overlooked by De Soto: the possibility that a household might use the land more efficiently for farming and livestock rearing and hence be able to create even more capital without risking losing the land through defaulting. It is important to note that, for the most part, small producers need the security of their land and not alien capital that is created from it. For these small producers, land is the only reliable asset they have for survival and they may need to protect it for the foreseeable future. However, we do not wish to sound as if we are advocating protection of small property to the point of arresting social change.

The problem with ITR and using land as collateral lies in the fact that many rural people do not have the entrepreneurial skills to use loans to create more capital and to service their debts so as to avoid foreclosure. To this extent, land mortgaging may serve as an instrument for disinheriting small producers (Shivji 2003 and 2004).

Selected Cases Reflecting the Agrarian Question in Tanzania
Conflicts over land and other natural resources offer the best reflection of the agrarian question in Tanzania. Besides the nature of law and policies on land and other natural resources,

grievances and struggles for access to the same reflect the profound roots of social and economic polarization among poor peasants, pastoralists and all local communities. Conflicts and disputes cut across different levels and groups of people, including local populations (particularly artisanal and small-scale miners) and mining companies, pastoralists and farmers, and even the state and indigenous peoples.

Artisanal and Small-Scale Miners versus Mining Companies

Land with mineral potential is one of the most significant areas of conflict between artisanal and small-scale miners (and local communities) and mining companies. Incidents of displacement, dislocation and compulsory acquisition of local community land for mining operations in the name of investment has given rise to various conflicts, social disruptions and human rights abuses.

Senga (2007:12-13) notes that the economic reforms of the 1990s resulted in the mushrooming of large-scale mining activities in Tanzania. Foreign investors were invited to enter the country's mining sector, and since the late 1990s Tanzania has witnessed so-called 'large foreign capital inflows'. The country's leaders vociferously encouraged foreign direct investment in mining to meet the conditions set out in a paper by the World Bank. The bank wanted the Tanzanian government to change the focus of its mineral policy from what it described as outdated mining to modern large-scale mining. Elaborating on that call for investments in mining, at the official opening of the AFGEM Tanzanite mine then President Benjamin William Mkapa was heard to state: "I invite you to Tanzania. Let us forge a profitable and smart partnership – we, in Tanzania with our mineral resources and you, with your capital, technology, know-how and managerial skills ... " Moreover, the then permanent secretary in the Ministry of Energy and Minerals, Arthur Mwakapugi, was also reported as saying: "The government will continue to attract foreign investments into the country, build a stronger partnership with mining investors and assure them that Tanzania is indeed an excellent destination for mining investments ..." [8]

In this milieu, Senga (2007) states that the extractive sector reforms and activities continue to have an clear bias towards reinforcing corporate power and interests rather than catalysing self-sustaining, self-reliant national economic recovery and development in a sustained environmental and human rights framework (politics enforcing economic structures). The result has been the entrenchment of the peripheral status the country's minerals, of poverty and of the marginalization of large populations living on the fringes of these resources. There were expectations that government would use the ('large') taxes accrued from mining to modernize peasant agriculture. However, the expected investment in agriculture is not evident and instead some peasants have lost their lands to mining companies.

Large-scale mining establishments in Tanzania with large investments included Kahama Mining and Bulyanhulu Gold Mine (owned by the Canadian company Barrick, the third largest gold company in the world), Afrika Mashariki Gold Mines, Golden Pride Project, Buhemba Gold Mine, Mererani Mining, Geita Gold Mine and Williamson Diamonds Min-

8. When addressing a mining sector consultative meeting in Dar es Salaam, Mwakapugi stated that in an attempt to attract more mining investors to the country, the government had been trying to give fair treatment to companies that undertook the ventures and urged the miners in turn to exploit this favourable stand. He further stated that the presence of large-scale mining companies within local communities has to an extent been a catalyst for improvements in rural life, through the mines' development and upgrading of infrastructure (for more details, see *The Guardian*, 3 July 2006).

ing. With the exception of Williamson Diamonds, which has a long history in Tanzania, the other companies commenced mining exploration in Tanzania from the 1990s in response to a formal invitation by the Tanzanian government. Although apologists of large-scale mining have always hailed the industry for its so-called "potential contribution to foreign exchange earnings", nothing or little is said about such earnings meeting local and national social needs. Above all, perennial disputes, conflicts and clashes have characterized the relationship between mining companies and local communities. Reports show that corporate mining in Tanzania has been responsible for the displacement, marginalization and impoverishment of some peasants and artisanal and small-scale miners.

The Citizen (26 February 2007:2)[9] reported that in Kahama, for example, the worst conflict was in August 1996 when about 50 artisanal and small-scale miners were alleged to have been buried alive by bulldozers of the Kahama Mining Company under the supervision of the police and Shinyanga regional authorities. Chachage has noted (2005:18-19) that about 30,000 artisanal miners were removed in 1998 and 1999 to make way for the construction of the Nzega and Geita gold mines. He also stated that there are unresolved conflicts between the South African gemstone miner AFGEM and thousands of artisanal and small-scale miners at Mererani in Arusha, which have often led to bloody confrontations between the two parties.[10]

It is further reported by Senga (2007:34-5) that clashes have been observed in various areas following the intensification of large-scale mining activities. Recent coverage by local newspapers, for example, highlights the conflict between artisanal and small-scale miners and mining companies. *Nipashe* (29 November 2006:1-4) carried a story about the clashes at Geita Gold Mines in Mwanza arising from villagers' grievances over dynamite blasting by the mining company. In those clashes, a Land Cruiser owned by the mining company was set ablaze immediately after the dynamite blast at the hill, which is very close to Katoma, a hamlet of approximately 500 people. It was alleged that the blasts badly injured two villagers while they were farming and that villagers used traditional weapons and stones when confronted by mineowners and workers. The clashes were stopped by the Field Force Unit (FFU), which used teargas to disperse the villagers.

---

9. Richard Mgamba "Artisanal Miners create work, wealth for local population". Apart from the Kahama incident, the author also reported clashes between villagers and police in August 2001 at Nyamongo Gold Mine. He stated that the clashes occurred when hundreds of small-scale miners protested their eviction to pave the way for the construction of Afrika Mashariki Gold Mine.

10. In another paper entitled All that Glitters must be Plundered (Mining Accumulation in Tanzania. Chachage provides several examples of recent conflicts. In 2001, AFGEM guards set dogs on miners and allegedly shot some of them. Over 50,000 small-scale miners in Mwabomba area in the Bukombe district of Shinyanga region have been battling a British mining company, Twigg Gold Exploration, which was granted areas previously in the hands of small-scale miners. In Tarime district, Mara region, over 10,000 villagers and artisanal miners from the Nyamongo area were rendered homeless when the Australian-owned Afrika Mashariki Gold Mines started its activities in the Nyabigena and Nyabirama areas in 2001. According to Chachage, the people were removed with the assistance of the Tanzania government's Field Force Unit (FFU), because according to him, there is a permanent FFU unit stationed in the area, and paid for by the company.

The Guardian (26 February 2007:1)[11] also reported that several people in Geita,[12] including small-scale miners, some 'unlicensed', set fire to a Scania lorry valued at about Tshs. 400 million and belonging to KASCCO, which had been hired by IAMGOLD [T] to deliver earth-moving machinery for use in covering mines excavated by artisanal and small-scale miners in villages surrounding the investor's area of operation. It was reported that the villagers had blockaded the road throughout the day, apparently to stop the passage of vehicles en route to Kahama Mining Company, allegedly to dump toxic soil.

Although the Mineral Policy (URT 1997) and the Mining Act (URT 1998), for example, specifically stipulate the need for government to improve the livelihoods of artisanal and small-scale miners, the Mineral Policy of Tanzania (1997:8) emphasizes that government policy for mineral sector development aims at attracting the private sector and enabling it to take the lead in exploration, mining development, mineral beneficiation and marketing. Despite the seemingly positive initiatives offered in the Report of the Presidential Committee to Review and Advise Government on Management of the Mineral Sector, the policy and the act still espouse and enforce existing colonial policies and acts regarding mining, which favour capitalist accumulation and lead to the perpetuation of the agrarian question.

Pastoralists versus Farmers

'Environmental scarcity', brought about in part by population growth and resultant environmental degradation, is considered by many scholars to be the driving force behind conflicts between pastoralists (or herders) and farmers (Baechler 1998; Homer-Dixon 1999; Kahl 2006). However, this paper argues that in order to understand the root causes of such conflicts, it is vital to examine the policy and historical context. We therefore need to trace the history of land use and villagization along with the policies and acts related to land tenure and pastoralism. This requires a political ecology approach.

One of the most tragic conflicts between pastoralists and peasant farmers, culminating in the death of 38 peasant farmers on 8 December 2000, happened in Kilosa district in Morogoro. According to Benjaminsen et al. (2009:434), the main event in this conflict took place in Rudewa Mbuyuni village at around 5 a.m., when several Maasai warriors attacked the village, killing 38 villagers and wounding many others. Following this tragic event, the Kilosa district commissioner was sacked and the local police commander was demoted and transferred. A number of Maasai *morans* and elders were arrested, some being kept in prison for up to 18 months, with one dying in prison. However, none was tried in court.

A key factor in the conflict was a border dispute on the floodplain between Twatwatwa and Rudewa Mbuyuni. The pastoralists argued that farmers were extending their irrigated fields into the wetlands that lie on Twatwatwa land, and the farmers insisted that herders let their livestock graze in their fields (Benjaminsen et al. 2009:439). Benjaminsen argues that the violence in Kilosa cannot be explained solely in terms of competition for scarce resources: it was more than just a resource conflict induced by a rising population. In fact,

---

11. A lead story entitled *Team to assess nation's mineral wealth* by Renatus Masuguliko, PST, Geita.

12. Following the intensification of LSM (Large Scale Mining) activities in Geita, a number of clashes and conflicts have been reported in that area. *The Citizen* (29 March, 2007:1:3), for instance, reported that hundreds of disgruntled Kalumwa and Nyamtukuza villagers in Msalala ward in Geita district had vandalized the main water pipe to the Bulyanhulu gold mine in protest at unfulfilled promises by mine authorities seven years earlier for them to access water from the same network. In the story, the mine's communications and public relations manager, Sauda Kilumanga, reportedly called the villagers' action very serious and discouraging.

while the human population is increasing in Kilosa, livestock numbers are not. Benjaminsen et al. established that there is a long history in Tanzania of modernization policies that marginalize pastoralists. This policy environment is gradually pushing pastoralists into a corner and making access to pastures and water in the dry season increasingly difficult.

Benjaminsen et al. (2009:441) explicitly argue that despite attempts to settle pastoralists in 'pastoral villages' and to make them adhere to calculated carrying capacities, Tanzanian pastoralists continue to practise a mobile, nomadic form of livestock keeping to maintain their livelihoods. For the authors, the villagization programme and land tenure and agricultural policies have favoured agriculture at the expense of livestock keeping, including loss of key dry season grazing resources. Recently, there have been reports of conflicts between pastoralists and farmers in districts such as Simanjiro, Tarime, Kiteto, Kilindi, Mbarali, Kilombero, Mahenge and in some districts of Manyara region, especially Hanang.

In respect of the Tanzanian Land Law and pastoralism, the unanswered questions posed by the Oxfam International Land Specialist can help us reflect on the power relations in the land and agrarian question as symbolized by the conflicts between pastoralists and farmers (Olenasha 2005). He asks: In what conditions can a collective customary right of occupancy be established on village common land? What is the scope in law for formal registration of a customary right of occupancy that is not 'exclusive'? How strong is the argument that only the village as a whole may hold title to common land within its boundaries? In what circumstances may a sub-group of people in the village, and in particular pastoralist land users, claim a customary right of occupancy to common land? How can the group be defined? What factors should determine membership of the group? What form/s of legal identity and constitution are likely to be most viable for the group? In particular, how can membership be constituted with enough flexibility to accommodate local demographic and livelihood changes? How can the rules of membership and operation of the group accommodate traditional decisionmaking on the use of the pastoral commons? In a group that includes pastoralists and non-pastoralists, how can rules of membership and operation of the group accommodate legitimate non-pastoral land-use rights, while safeguarding against fragmentation? Traditional communal land was not open to everybody and part of the current problem is the equating of 'communal' with 'open access'.

Reflection on Forms of Eviction and Displacement among Pastoral Communities

According to Oxfam (2008:3-4), over the past few decades greater pressure has been put on pastoralist grazing lands and water resources as populations have increased and grazing land has been taken for cultivation, conservation areas and state use. In Tanzania, conservation areas have led to more land being taken from pastoralists than all the other factors put together. About 95 per cent of Monduli district, which is in the heart of Maasailand, has been set aside for conservation, even though more than one-third of protected areas in Tanzania have traditionally belonged to pastoralist communities.

Oxfam further notes that livestock have been squeezed on to lands too small to sustain pastoral production, as pastoralists rely on freedom of movement to manage rangelands effectively. Key resource areas, for example dry-season grazing lands, are a target for agricultural use because of their productive potential. Once pastoralists lose these key areas, their whole strategy for dealing with drought is compromised. Furthermore, the livestock population is growing more slowly than the human population: livestock numbers in East

Africa have remained fairly constant over recent years because of epidemics and starvation associated with floods and recurrent drought. The result is that more pastoralists are reliant on fewer livestock. Resource competition significantly increases the risk of conflict between different groups of land users. This risk is greatest during times of stress, such as drought or floods, when available resources are even more restricted. Increasingly, many pastoralists can no longer rely on livestock alone to provide them with a livelihood, but other income-earning opportunities remain limited, as the growing number of destitute ex-pastoralists, who number in the thousands, shows.

In March 2006, the government issued an eviction order to pastoral communities in the Usangu/Ihefu basin in Mbarali district, Mbeya region. According to the Land Rights Research and Resources Institute, the eviction of pastoralists from Usangu and other parts of the country has always been carried out violently, without due regard to and respect for the human and land rights of livestock owners.[13] In fairness, it must be added that the government has allowed pastoralists to move to many new areas (including Bagamoyo district) traditionally not occupied by nomadic pastoralists.

Then Minister for Livestock Development Anthony Diallo, presenting his budget estimates for 2007-08, announced that of a total of 303,254[14] livestock scheduled for removal from Mbarali, 218,000 had actually moved: 100,000 to Chunya, 65,636 to Rufiji, 18,000 to Kilwa, 8,000 to Kisarawe, 4,958 to Lindi Rural, 4,000 to Kilombero, Ulanga and Kilosa, and 17,406 to Singida, Tabora, Dodoma, Rukwa and Ruvuma districts. In response, the opposition spokesperson, Mwadini Abbas Jecha, criticized the eviction process, citing the conclusions of the investigative report by PINGOs Forum and its partners. He called for compensation for the livestock keepers, and also for the completed report of the independent commission of inquiry (submitted to the president) to be made public and its recommendations implemented.

Inbuilt societal stereotypes and negative perceptions of pastoralists have often been the basis of policies, laws and orders that directly affect the majority of pastoral communities and their mode of livelihood. In some of these basic perceptions, they are characterized as destroyers of the environment, the source of animal diseases, enemies of wildlife heritage and practitioners of an economically unviable livelihood. Worse still, attitudes that have found their way into mainstream policies often go unchallenged, even when they are contradicted by scientific proof. So, the events in Usangu were basically expected because their basis was known, however wrongly framed, and even the consequences and ways of managing the issue were predetermined. The state employed and demonstrated excessive force in executing the initial eviction, without even directing the pastoralists where to relocate their stocks.

In July and August 2009, the media reported on the violent eviction of Maasai from their land in Loliondo in northern Tanzania, allegedly to enable the United Arab Emirates hunting company Otterlo Business Corporation (OBC) to carry out big game hunting. The

---

13. Brief article titled 'Pastoralists Survival Still at Stake … Here is a Sad Story of their Ruthless Eviction from Usangu Basin in Mbeya Tanzania'.

14. The figures are at odds with those given by the prime minister in April, when he told parliament that it had been estimated that 235,000 cattle should be removed from Ihefu (i.e., Usangu Game Reserve), but that a total of 303,354 had subsequently been removed from Mbarali district, 130,737 to Lindi region, 72,517 to Coast region, and 100,000 to Chunya district in Mbeya region (Tanzania Hansard, 9th Sitting of the7th Session of the 2005-10 Parliament, 20 April 2007, Speech on the Adjournment of Parliament, p. 98).

media (including television) showed how entire villages had been razed and their inhabitants forcibly evicted. Brutal beatings and rapes had reportedly taken place during the operation, which was carried out by Tanzania's riot police. After the operation, thousands of Maasai lacked shelter and they and their cattle were without food or water. Maasai attempting to return to their homes faced arrest and possible imprisonment. Immediately after the eviction, about 100 evicted Maasai marched on State House in Dar es Salaam demanding an audience with President Jakaya Kikwete. Their demand was refused. However, the Minister of Natural Resources and Tourism did announce an investigation into the forced evictions. Some observers have expressed concern that the government investigation will be a whitewash and have called for an independent inquiry.

Nelson (2005:8), citing Majamba (2001), has established that the allocation of these areas to hunting companies has not taken into account the land rights of the communities resident in the Game Controlled Areas (GCAs). The Wildlife Conservation Act (WCA) has a provision that hunting carried out on private lands requires the consent of the landowners, and titled or certified village lands qualify as private lands under the WCA. This consent has never been sought when allocating hunting concessions and in general local communities have no role in the block allocation process. The result is that tourist hunting is conducted extensively on community lands without the permission or involvement of the landholders. Some conflicts inevitably occur as a result of outsiders being granted access to village lands without the participation of the people living there. Hunting activities may conflict with livestock grazing, forest product collection or other local economic activities.

CONCLUSION AND RECOMMENDATIONS

Despite arguments by some scholars (for example, the 'internationalist left') that the agrarian question has been resolved because the peasantry is fast disappearing, the discussion and analysis set forth in this paper enable us to deduce that the agrarian question, as the national question, remains unresolved. The global process of imperialist accumulation of natural resources (including land) has perpetuated the agrarian crisis and underscores the need for the land question to be analysed in the context of the interactions between process and structure, between the role of the state – both colonial and contemporary – in defining land tenure and the alliances (both national and international) the state forms with capital, social classes and groups around the land question.

As noted earlier, conflicts over land and other natural resources offer the best reflection of the agrarian question in Tanzania. The 1999 land laws give too much power to the government in allocating land. Even the land settled by peasants and pastoralists for many generations belongs to the government. The people should have full control of their own land (for example, through freehold). The government has its own land which is more abundant than the peasants' and pastoralists' land.

The political economy of the agrarian question has shown how development of the capitalist mode of production and the global process of imperialist accumulation have been dependent on the dispossession of part of the peasantry in Tanzania, as the cases discussed in this paper have revealed. Local communities have been left destitute and impoverished and have been exposed to massive displacement and dispossession, all instigated by neoliberal economic reforms in past decades and fully intensified by continuing forms of capital accumulation. The adoption of 'multi-occupations' by peasants shows how peasant labour super-exploits itself through labour intensification, thus turning the peasant sector into a reservoir of cheap labour. What we see is the failure of agrarian capitalism to develop, with the consequence that the upper levels of the peasantry move into commercial and merchant activities rather than becoming capitalist farmers.

'Poverty Reduction', 'Integrated Rural Development' and other development strategies entailed economic and agrarian policies which direct the use of land for extroverted (export) purposes, rather than for the national market and related industries. These policies and programmes repress agricultural productivity among the peasantry, leading to depressed wages and peasant incomes and, most importantly, pushing out smallholder farmers by encouraging large-scale private sector initiatives in the agrarian sector. As already noted, we believe the implication for the agrarian sector is that it really has to orient itself towards the market, which cannot be done with only the traditional cash crops of coffee, cotton, sisal and tea.

Kautsky's *Die Agrafrage* (1899) is the classic analysis of agriculture in societies dominated by peasants. Kautsky and Lenin were engaged in concrete investigations of rural economies in their presentations (Lenin followed Kautsky's work with his classic 'The Development of Capitalism in Russia') on the agrarian/rural question. Both Kautsky and Lenin overestimated the speed of the development of capitalism in the countryside. As we have seen in this paper, most rural dwellers are still peasants and capitalist agriculture has barely developed. Nevertheless, it is the peasant who is creative, able to hire labour, find good markets, invest in technology, access credit and accumulates land and other resources such as animals, who will move up socially and economically. Primitive accumulation is taking place and the expansion of and further invasion by global capitalist companies is almost unstoppable, as peasants lack political power, and the local state remains weak, displaying the unstable characteristics and weaknesses of a petty-bourgeois state. Nevertheless (as Lenin and Kautsky would have argued), social and economic change cannot be arrested. We can, in conclusion, support the growth of nurture capitalism in Tanzania, which is in line with the evolution of a powerful local agrarian class. The concept of nurture capitalism was coined by Schatz (1988) when he attempted to construct a typological classification of African capitalism after independence in the 1960s.

Schatz identified a type of capitalism called piracy, in which state revenues can be directly tapped for corrupt private gain. Pirate capitalism is an orientation in which control of the state is used to increase private incomes and wealth (Schatz 1988: 66-7). Kickbacks are paid on government contracts and loans are made that need not be repaid. Piracy also involves the corrupt bestowal by the government of strategic economic positions upon favoured private citizens. Nevertheless, this is done not primarily through subsidizing and aiding productive activities, but through corruption in one form or another. The typical example in the 1970s and 1980s was the allocation of foreign exchange. A current example is the allocation of contracts and licences. An import licence for rice, wheat or maize is issued when the domestic price of rice is a multiple of the international price and the importer is exempted from some or all taxes. This ends up as a licence to make a future.

Another type of capitalism identified in Africa by Schatz is nurture capitalism. In this kind of capitalism, the government assists and nurtures private productive activities. The state provides tariff protection, low interest loans, subsidized industrial estates, preferential government purchasing programmes, and technical and commercial advice and assistance. When such programmes are successful, they nurture growth. Under nurture capitalism, assistance to productive activities (including agriculture) predominates, while under pirate capitalism piracy predominates.

Nurture capitalism is an orientation whereby the state undertakes to accelerate economic development by nurturing private business engaged in productive activities such as agriculture and industry. Here the acquisition of state-controlled surplus is associated to a significant degree with productive activities.

Schatz (1988:66) observed that the record of nurture capitalism in Africa has not been good. Pirate capitalism had the upper hand, and under it development is more likely to stagnate than under nurture capitalism. The two types can and do coexist. The version of capitalism which predominates in a particular country depends on several conditions, such as the prior existence or absence of a substantial capitalist class when the transfer of power occurs (Schatz 1988:66).

The third type of capitalism identified in Africa is termed ambivalent capitalism (Schatz 1988:67), defined as the form of capitalism with an overlay of anti-capitalist rhetoric and feeling. Here there is both reliance on and antagonism towards capitalism. Schatz views this tendency as capitalism that shoots itself in the foot. Little is done to promote private business in the directly productive sector of the economy, and government actions may even be an impediment. Ambivalent capitalism characterized Afro-Marxist and populist socialist regimes in Africa.

In the 1960s, the Tanzania state supported nurture capitalism. However, from 1967 for about 20 years the state favoured ambivalent capitalism, which ruined the peasant economy to the point that it came to fit a Chayanovian or moral economic characterization. Currently under neoliberalism, aspects of piracy are evident. Within the state there are members of the ruling elite who are inclined to piracy and those who are inclined to nurture capitalism. A touch of populism is always there. However, in the class struggle, Tanzanian scholars should support the (weak) nurture capitalist faction to defeat the pirates. Pirates tend to fall more in line with the primitive accumulation mentioned in the paper, which they pursue in alliance with their international associates, who are the global corporations now mining and carrying out all sorts of business in Tanzania.

In order to stimulate further research into the agrarian question, this paper recommends the following five topics;

- The history and dynamics of land tenure systems;
- The impact of agrarian change on Tanzanian rural households;
- The nature and character of Tanzanian peasant exploitation and the agrarian question;
- The global process of imperialist accumulation of natural resources;
- Why is the green revolution elusive in Tanzania? and
- Reconsidering the agrarian question: Discourses and debates from an African perspective.

The recommended topics, which have been introduced and generally discussed in this paper, are expected to provide a foundation for further research and to act as a catalyst for debates on the problem at hand.

REFERENCES

AFGEM (African Gem Resources Limited) (2002) *Annual Report.*

AGRA (2007) Agra-alliance, www.agra-alliance.

Amin, S. (1972) *Theory of Imperialism*. London: Longman.

Anderson, D and V. Broch-Due (2006) "The Poor are not us: Poverty and Pastoralism", *Eastern African Studies*. Dar es Salaam: Mkuki na Nyo; Kampala: Fountain; Nairobi: E.A.E.P; Oxford: James Currey; and Athens: Ohio University Press.

Araghi, F. (1995) "Global De-Peasantization, 1945-1990", *Sociological Quarterly* 36(2):337- 68.

— (2000) "The Great Global Enclosure of Our Times: Peasants and the Agrarian Question at the End of the Twentieth Century" in F. Magdoff, J.B. Bellamy Foster and F.H. Buttel (eds), *Hungry for Profit: The Agribusiness Threat to Farmers, Food and the Environment*. New York: Monthly Review.

Baechler, G. (1998) *Violence through Environmental Discrimination. Causes, Rwanda Arena, and Conflict Model*. Dordrecht, Boston and London: Kluwer.

Baland, J.-M. and J-P. Platteau (1996) *Halting Degradation of Natural Resources. Is there a Role for Rural Communities?* Oxford: Clarendon Press.

Benjaminsen, T, F. Maganga and J. Abdallah (2009) "The Kilosa Killings: Political Ecology of a Farmer-Herder Conflict in Tanzania", *Development and Change* 40 (3):423-45.

Berlin, I. (1979) *Against the Current: Essays in the History of Ideas*. Pimlico: Hogarth.

Bernstein, H. (1977) "Notes on Capital and Peasantry", *Review of African Political Economy* 10 (Sep.-Dec. 1977):60-73.

— (1981) "Notes on State and Peasantry: The Tanzanian Case", *Review of African Political Economy* 21 (May-Sep.):44-62.

— (1996/7) "Agrarian Questions. Essays in Appreciation of T.J. Byres", Special Issue of *Journal of Peasant Studies* 24 (1/2).

— (2002) "Land Reform: Taking a Long(er) View", *Journal of Agrarian Change* 2(4):433-63.

— (2004) "Changing Before Our Very Eyes", *Journal of Agrarian Change* 4(1-2).

— (2005) "Rural Land and Land Conflicts in Sub- Saharan Africa" in S. Moyo and P. Yeros (eds), *Reclaiming the Land: The Resurgence of Rural Movements in Africa, Asia and Latin America*. London and Cape Town: Zed and David Philip.

Bernstein, H. and T. Byers (2001) "From Peasants Studies to Agrarian Change", *Journal of Agrarian Change* 1:1-56.

Berry, S. (1993) *No Condition is Permanent: Social Dynamics of Agrarian Change in Sub- Saharan Africa*. Madison: University of Wisconsin Press.

Bryceson, D.F. (2000) "African Peasants' Centrality and Marginality: Rural Labour Transformations", in D. Bryceson, C. Kay, and J. Mooij (eds), *Disappearing Peasantries? Rural Labor in Africa, Asia and Latin America*. London: Intermediate Technology Publications.

Byres, T.J. (1991) "The Agrarian Question and Differing Forms of Capitalist Transition: An Essay with Reference to Asia", in J. Breman and S. Mundle (eds), *Rural Transformation in Asia*. Delhi: Oxford University Press.

— (1996) *Capitalism from Above and Capitalism from Below. An Essay in Comparative Political Economy.* London: Macmillan.

Cabral, A. (1979) *Unity and Struggle.* New York: Monthly Review Press.

Callaghy, T.M. (1988) "The State and the Development of Capitalism in Africa: Theoretical, Historical, and Comparative Reflections", in D. Rothchild and N. Chazan (eds), *The Precarious Balance: State and Society in Africa.* Boulder CO, and London: Westview.

Calvert, A. (1917) *German East Africa.* London: T. Werner Lawrie.

Chachage, C.S.L. (2005) "Can Africa's Poor Inherit the Earth and all its Mineral Rights?" Paper Presented at the CODESRIA General Assembly, Maputo, 5-12 December.

Chayanov, A.V. (1991) [1919]. *The Theory of Peasant Co-operatives.* London: IB Tauris.

— (1966) [1925]. *The Theory of Peasant Economy.* D. Thorner, B. Kerblay and R.E.F. Smith (eds). Homewood IL: Irwin.

Chimhowu, A. and P. Woodhouse (2006) "Customary vs Private Property Rights? Dynamics and Trajectories of Vernacular Land Markets in Sub-Saharan Africa", *Journal of Agrarian Change* 6(3):346-71.

Coulson, A. (1977) "Agricultural Policies in Mainland Tanzania", *Review of African Political Economy* 10 (Sept.-Dec.).

De Janvry, A. (1981) *The Agrarian Question and Reformism in Latin America.* Baltimore: Johns Hopkins University Press.

Edigheji, O. (2006) "The Emerging South African Democratic Developmental State and the People's Contract". Johannesburg: Centre for Policy Studies. Mimeo.

Fanon, F. (1967) *The Wretched of the Earth.* C. Farrington (trans.). London: Penguin.

Fernandes, B.M. (2001) "The Occupation as a Form of Access to Land". Paper prepared for delivery at the XXIII International Congress of the Latin American Studies Association, Washington DC, 6-8 September.

Forster, P.G. and S. Maghimbi (eds) (1992) *The Tanzanian Peasantry: Economy in Crisis.* Aldershot, Brookfield USA, Hong Kong, Singapore and Sidney: Avebury

Freyhold, M. (1979) *Ujamaa Villages in Tanzania: An Analysis of a Social Experiment.* London: Heinemann.

Friedmann, H. (1993) The Political Economy of Food: A Global Crisis. *New Left Review* 197:29-57.

Gibbon, P. and M. Neocosmos (1985) "Some Problems in the Political Economy of African Socialism", in H. Bernstein and B.K. Campbell (eds), *Contradictions of Accumulation in Africa: Studies in Economy and State.* Beverly Hills CA: Sage.

Ghimire, K. (ed.) (2001) *Whose Land? Civil Perspectives on Land Reform and Rural Poverty Reduction: Regional Experiences from Africa, Asia and Latin America.* Geneva: UNRIDS.

Glover, D. and T. Lim (1992) *Contract Farming in Southeast Asia: Three Country Studies.* University of Malaya: Institute for Advanced Studies.

Hall, R. (2007) "Policy Options 1: Land Use and Livelihoods in South Africa's Land Reform". PLASS and ICCO: Another Countryside? Policy Options for Land and Agrarian Reform in South Africa, Somerset West, 24-25 October.

Hardin, G. (1968) "Tragedy of the Commons", *Science* 162(3859) (13 Dec.): 1243-1248.

Harvey, D. (2003) *The New Imperialism*. Oxford: Oxford University Press.

— (2005) *A Brief History of Neoliberalism*. Oxford: Oxford University Press.

Homer-Dixon, T. (1999) *Environment, Scarcity, and Violence*. Princeton NJ: Princeton University Press.

Hyden, G. and M. Bretton (eds) (1992) *Governance and Politics in Africa*. Boulder CO and London: Lynne Rienner.

Iane, P.A. (1984) "The State of the Tanzanian Economy". University of Dar es Salaam, Economic Research Bureau, Paper No. 84:1.

Ikdahl, I. (2008) "Go Home and Clear the Conflict: Human Rights Perspectives on Gender and Land in Tanzania", in B. Englert and E. Daley (eds), *Women's Land Rights and Privatization in Eastern Africa*. Suffolk: James Currey.

Izumi, K. (1999) "Liberalization, Gender, and the Land Question in Sub-Saharan Africa", *Gender and Development* 7(3)(Nov.).

Kahl, C. (2006) *States, Scarcity, and Civil Strife in the Developing World*. Princeton NJ: Princeton University Press.

Kamata, N. (2003) Usuli na Muktadha wa Mapendekezo ya Marekebisho ya Sheria za Ardhi Mada iliyowasilishwa Kwenye Kongamano juu ya Uwekezaji, Ubinafishaji and Haki za Ardhi za Wazalishaji Wadogowadogo Tanzania. Baraza la Maaskofu-Kurasini (TEC) Tarehe, 21-22 Feb.

Kautsky, K. (1899) *Die Agrafrage*. Stuttgart: Dietz.

Kimario, A.M. (1992) *Marketing Cooperatives in Tanzania*. Dar es Salaam: Dar es Salaam University Press.

Kuba, R. and C. Lentz. (eds) (2006) *Land and the Politics of Belonging in West Africa*. Leiden: Brill.

Lenin, V.I. ([1899] 1956) *The Development of Capitalism in Russia*. Moscow: Foreign Language Publishing House.

Little, P. and M. Watts (eds) (1994) *Living under Contract: Contract Farming and Agrarian Transformation in Sub-Saharan Africa*. Madison: University of Wisconsin Press.

Loftchie, M.F. (1978) "Agrarian Crisis and Economic Liberalization in Tanzania", *Journal of Modern African Studies* 16(3).

Luxemburg, R. (1951) [1913] *The Accumulation of Capital*. London: Routledge and Kegan Paul.

Mafeje, A. (2003) *The Agrarian Question, Access to Land and Peasant Responses in Sub- Saharan Africa*. Geneva: United Nations Research Institute for Social Development.

Maghimbi, S. (1990) "Rural Development Policy and Planning in Tanzania". Unpublished PhD Thesis. University of London (London School of Economics).

— (1995) "The Rise and Fall of Nyerere's Populism (Ujamaa)", in P.G. Forster and S. Maghimbi (eds), *The Tanzanian Peasantry: Further Studies*. Aldershot: Avebury.

— (1999a) "Some Population Problems in Bagamoyo District", in K.M. Howell and A.K. Semesi (eds), *Coastal Resources of Bagamoyo District, Tanzania*. Dar es Salaam: Faculty of Science, University of Dar es Salaam.

— (1999b) "The Failure of Institutional, Technical and Structural Shifts in Tanzanian Peasant Agriculture: Some Lessons from India's Green Revolution", in P.G. Forster and S. Maghimbi (eds), *Agrarian Economy, State and Society in Contemporary Tanzania*. Aldershot: Ashgate.

— (2003) "Land Tenure Reform as an Instrument of Better Resource Use: A Case Study of Nomads in the Drylands of Northern and Central Tanzania", in H. Oyieke et al. (eds), *Sustainable Biodiversity Management for Reduced Community Vulnerability to Drought*. Nairobi: Regional Programme for Sustainable Use of Dry Land Biodiversity.

— (2007) "Recent Changes in Crop Patterns in the Kilimanjaro Region of Tanzania: The Decline of Coffee and Rise of Maize and Rice", *African Study Monographs*, Supplementary Issue 35:73-85.

Majamba, H.I. (2001) *Regulating the Hunting Industry in Tanzania: Reflections on the Legislative, Institutional and Policy-making Frameworks*. Lawyers' Environmental Action Team Research Report No. 4. Dar es Salaam: LEAT.

Mamdani, M. (2001) *When Victims Become Killers: Colonialism, Nativism, and the Genocide in Rwanda*. Princeton: Princeton University Press.

Mapolu, H. (1990) "Tanzania: Imperialism, the State and the Peasantry", in Hamid Ait Amara and B. Founou-Tchuigoua (eds), *African Agriculture: The Critical Choices*. Tokyo: United Nations University Press; London and New Jersey: Zed.

McCarthy, D.M.P. (1982) *Colonial Bureaucracy and Creating Underdevelopment: Tanganyika 1914-1940*. Aines: Iowa University Press.

McHenry, D.E. Jr (1979) *Tanzania's Ujamaa Villages: The Implementation of a Rural Development Strategy*. Berkeley: Institute of International Studies.

McMichael, P. (1984) *Settlers and the Agrarian Question: Capitalism in Colonial Australia*. Cambridge: Cambridge University Press.

— (1997) "Rethinking Globalization: The Agrarian Question Revisited", *Review of International Political Economy* 4(4)(Winter):630-62.

— (2007) "Reframing Development: Global Peasant Movements and the New Agrarian Question", *Revista Nera* 10:27-40.

— (2008) "Peasants Make their Own History, but not Just as they Please", *Journal of Agrarian Change* 8 (2 and 3) (Apr. and July):205-28.

Mduma, J.K. (2006) *Rural Off-Farm Employment and its Effects on Adoption of Labor Intensive Soil Conserving Measures in Tanzania*. Frankfurt am Main: Lang.

Mkandawire, T. and C. Soludo (1999) *African Perspectives on Structural Adjustment: Our Continent, Our Future*. Dakar: CODESRIA, IDRC and AWP.

Moore, J. (2008) "Ecological Crises and the Agrarian Question in World-Historical Perspective", *Monthly Review* (Nov).

Moyo, S. (2001) "The Land Occupation Movement and Democratization in Zimbabwe: Contradictions of Neoliberalism", *Millennium: Journal of International Studies* 30(2):311-30.

— (2004) "The Land and Agrarian Question in Zimbabwe". Paper presented at the Conference on The Agrarian Constraint and Poverty Reduction: Macroeconomic Lessons for Africa, Addis Ababa, 17-18 December.

— (2007) "Land in the Political Economy of African Development: Alternative Strategies for Reform", *Africa Development* XXXII (4):1-34.

— (2008) *African Land Questions, Agrarian Transitions and the State: Contradictions of Neoliberal Land Reforms*. Dakar: CODESRIA.

Moyo, S. and P. Yeros (2007) "The Resurgence of Rural Movements under Neoliberalism", in S. Moyo and P. Yeros (eds), *Reclaiming the Land: The Resurgence of Rural Movements in Africa, Asia and Latin America*. London: Zed and Cape Town: David Philip.

— (2004b) "Land Occupations and Land Reform in Zimbabwe: Towards the National Democratic Revolution", in S. Moyo and P. Yeros (eds), *Reclaiming the Land: The Resurgence of Rural Movements in Africa, Asia and Latin America*. London: Zed and Cape Town: David Philip.

Mwamila, B., K. Kulindwa, O. Kibazohi, H. Majamba, H. Mlinga, D. Charlz, M. Chijoriga, A. Temu, G. John, R.P.C. Temu, S. Maliondo, M.S. Nchimbi, Z. Mvena and J. Lupala (2009), "Feasibility of Large Scale Bio-fuel Production in Tanzania". Study report submitted to the Swedish Embassy in Tanzania.

Nelson, F. (2005) "Wildlife Management and Village Land Tenure in Northern Tanzania". TNRF. Occasional Paper No. 6. Paper prepared for the land symposium held in Dar es Salaam, March 1 and 2.

Nyerere, J.K. (1967) *Socialism and Rural Development*. Dar es Salaam: Government Printers.

Olenasha, W. (2005) "Reforming Land Tenure in Tanzania: For Whose Benefit?" A study undertaken for HakiArdhi, Dar es Salaam. www.hakiardhi.or.tz

Oxfam International (2008) "Survival of the Fittest: Pastoralism and Climate Change in East Africa". Oxfam Briefing Paper 116.

Pallotti, A. (2008) "Tanzania: Decentralising Power or Spreading Poverty?" *Review of African Political Economy* 116:221-35.

Peters, P. (2004) "At the Risk of Being Heard: Identity, Indigenous Rights, and Postcolonial States (review)", *Anthropological Quarterly* 77(2)(Spring):375-80.

Petras, J. and H. Veltmeyer (2001) *Globalization Unmasked: Imperialism in the 21st Century*. London: Zed.

Platteau, J-P. (1992) "Small Scale Fisheries and the Evolutionist Theory of Institutional Development", in I. Tvedten and B. Hersoug (eds), *Fishing for Development: Small-Scale Fisheries in Africa*. Uppsala: Scandinavian Institute of African Studies.

— (2000) *Institutions, Social Norms and Economic Development*. Amsterdam: Harwood Academic.

Rukuni M., P. Tawonenzi, E.K. Eicher, M. Munyuki-Hungwe and P. Matondi (eds) (2006) *Zimbabwe's Agricultural Revolution Revisited*. Harare: University of Zimbabwe Publications.

Schatz, S.P. (1988) "African Capitalism and African Economic Performance", in H. Glickman (ed.), *The Crisis and Challenge of African Development*. New York: Greenwood.

Senga, M.A. (2007) "Accumulation by Dispossession and Displacement: Some Reflections from Epanko Mines, Ulanga District, Morogoro". Unpublished MA Dissertation. University of Dar es Salaam.

Shanin, T. (1971) *Peasants and Peasant Societies*. Harmondsworth: Penguin.

Shivji, I.G. (1975) "Peasants and Class Alliances", *Review of African Political Economy* 3(May-Oct.):10-18

— (1976) *Class Struggles in Tanzania*. New York and London: Monthly Review Press.

— (1987) "The Roots of Agrarian Crisis in Tanzania: A Theoretical Perspective", *Eastern Africa Social Science Research Review* III(1):111-34.

— (1998) *Not Yet Democracy: Reforming Land Tenure in Tanzania*. London: IIED; Dar es Salaam: HAKIARDHI/Faculty of Law, University of Dar es Salaam.

— (1999) "The Land Acts 1999: A Cause for Celebration or a Celebration of a Cause?" Keynote Address to the Workshop on Land held at Morogoro, 19-20 February.

— (2003) Ubinafsishaji and Ugenishaji wa Ardhi: Je ni Ukombozi wa Mnyonge au Unyonge wa Wakombozi? *Mada iliyowasilishwa kwenye Kongamano juu ya Uwekezaji, Ubinafsishaji na Haki za Ardhi za Wazalishaji Wadogo Wadogo Tanzania*. Baraza la Maaskofu-Kurasini (TEC), Tarehe 21-22 February.

— (2009a) *Accumulation in an African Periphery: A Theoretical Framework*. Dar es Salaam: Mkuki na Nyota Publishers.

— (2009b) *Where is Uhuru? Reflections on the Struggle for Democracy in Africa*. In G. Murunga (ed.) Cape Town, Dakar, Nairobi and Oxford: Fahamu Books.

Stalin, J.V (1954) *The Agrarian Question*. Moscow: Foreign Languages Publishing House.

Sulle, E. and F. Nelson. (2009) *Bio-fuels, Land Access and Rural Livelihoods in Tanzania*. London: IIED.

Tanganyika Government (1953) *Government Circular No. 4.*

Tenga, R.W. (1987) "Land Law and the Peasantry in Tanzania: A Review of the Post-Arusha Period", *Eastern Africa Social Science Research Review* III(1):38-57.

University Press of Africa (for Ministry of Information and Tourism, United Republic of Tanzania) (1968) *Tanzania Today*. Nairobi.

URT (United Republic of Tanzania) (1994) *Report of the Presidential Commission of Inquiry into Land Matters*. Vol I. Dar es Salaam: Ministry of Lands, Housing and Urban Development in Cooperation with the Nordic Institute of African Studies.

— (1997) *The Mineral Policy of Tanzania*. Ministry of Energy and Minerals.

— (1999) *The Land Act, No, 4 of 1999*. Dar es Salaam.

— (2003) *Population and Housing Census General Report*. Central Census Office, National Bureau of Statistics. Dar es Salaam: Government Printer.

— (2005) *Strategic Plan for the Implementation of the Land Laws*. Dar es Salaam: Ministry of Lands and Human Settlements Development.

— (2009) *Kilimo Kwanza* (Agriculture First): Mapinduzi ya Kijani (The Green Revolution).

Woodhouse, P., H. Bernstein and D. Hulme (2000) *African Enclosures? The Social Dynamics*. Oxford: James Currey.

World Bank (1983) *Report No.4052-TA: Tanzania Agricultural Sector Report*. Washington DC.

World Development Report (2008) Agriculture for Development. Washington DC: World Bank.

Wuyts, M. (2008) *The Growth-Poverty Nexus in Tanzania from a Developmental Perspective*. Research for Poverty Alleviation (REPOA) Special Paper No. 8. Dar es Salaam: Mkuki na Nyota.

Yeros, P. (2002) "Zimbabwe and the Dilemmas of the Left", *Historical Materialism* 10(2):3-15.

CURRENT AFRICAN ISSUES PUBLISHED BY THE INSTITUTE
Recent issues in the series are available electronically
for download free of charge www.nai.uu.se

1. *South Africa, the West and the Frontline States. Report from a Seminar.*1981, 34 pp

2. Maja Naur, *Social and Organisational Change in Libya.* 1982, 33 pp

3. *Peasants and Agricultural Production in Africa. A Nordic Research Seminar. Follow-up Reports and Discussions.* 1981, 34 pp

4. Ray Bush & S. Kibble, *Destabilisation in Southern Africa, an Overview.* 1985, 48 pp

5. Bertil Egerö, *Mozambique and the Southern African Struggle for Liberation.* 1985, 29 pp

6. Carol B.Thompson, *Regional Economic Polic under Crisis Condition. Southern African Development.*1986, 34 pp

7. Inge Tvedten, *The War in Angola, Internal Conditions for Peace and Recovery.* 1989, 14 pp

8. Patrick Wilmot, *Nigeria's Southern Africa Policy 1960–1988.* 1989, 15 pp

9. Jonathan Baker, *Perestroika for Ethiopia: In Search of the End of the Rainbow?* 1990, 21 pp

10. Horace Campbell, *The Siege of Cuito Cuanavale.* 1990, 35 pp

11. Maria Bongartz, *The Civil War in Somalia. Its genesis and dynamics.* 1991, 26 pp

12. S.B.O. Gutto, *Human and People's Rights in Africa. Myths, Realities and Prospects.* 1991, 26 pp

13. Said Chikhi, Algeria. *From Mass Rebellion to Workers' Protest.* 1991, 23 pp

14. Bertil Odén, *Namibia's Economic Links to South Africa.* 1991, 43 pp

15. Cervenka Zdenek, *African National Congress Meets Eastern Europe. A Dialogue on Common Experiences.* 1992, 49 pp, ISBN 91-7106-337-4

16. Diallo Garba, Mauritania–The Other Apartheid? 1993, 75 pp, ISBN 91-7106-339-0

17. Zdenek Cervenka and Colin Legum, *Can National Dialogue Break the Power of Terror in Burundi?* 1994, 30 pp, ISBN 91-7106-353-6

18. Erik Nordberg and Uno Winblad, *Urban Environmental Health and Hygiene in Sub-Saharan Africa.* 1994, 26 pp, ISBN 91-7106-364-1

19. Chris Dunton and Mai Palmberg, *Human Rights and Homosexuality in Southern Africa.* 1996, 48 pp, ISBN 91-7106-402-8

20. Georges Nzongola-Ntalaja *From Zaire to the Democratic Republic of the Congo.* 1998, 18 pp, ISBN 91-7106-424-9

21. Filip Reyntjens, *Talking or Fighting? Political Evolution in Rwanda and Burundi, 1998–1999.* 1999, 27 pp, ISBN 91-7106-454-0

22. Herbert Weiss, *War and Peace in the Democratic Republic of the Congo.* 1999, 28 pp, ISBN 91-7106-458-3

23. Filip Reyntjens, *Small States in an Unstable Region – Rwanda and Burundi, 1999–2000,* 2000, 24 pp, ISBN 91-7106-463-X

24. Filip Reyntjens, *Again at the Crossroads: Rwanda and Burundi, 2000–2001.* 2001, 25 pp, ISBN 91-7106-483-4

25. Henning Melber, *The New African Initiative and the African Union. A Preliminary Assessment and Documentation.* 2001, 36 pp, ISBN 91-7106-486-9

26. Dahilon Yassin Mohamoda, *Nile Basin Cooperation. A Review of the Literature.* 2003, 39 pp, ISBN 91-7106-512-1

27. Henning Melber (ed.), *Media, Public Discourse and Political Contestation in Zimbabwe.* 2004, 39 pp, ISBN 91-7106-534-2

28. Georges Nzongola-Ntalaja, *From Zaire to the Democratic Republic of the Congo. Second and Revised Edition.* 2004, 23 pp, ISBN-91-7106-538-5

29. Henning Melber (ed.), *Trade, Development, Cooperation – What Future for Africa?* 2005, 44 pp, ISBN 91-7106-544-X

30. Kaniye S.A. Ebeku, *The Succession of Faure Gnassingbe to the Togolese Presidency – An International Law Perspective.* 2005, 32 pp, ISBN 91-7106-554-7

31. Jeffrey V. Lazarus, Catrine Christiansen, Lise Rosendal Østergaard, Lisa Ann Richey, *Models for Life – Advancing antiretroviral therapy in sub-Saharan Africa.* 2005, 33 pp, ISBN 91-7106-556-3

32. Charles Manga Fombad and Zein Kebonang, *AU, NEPAD and the APRM – Democratisation Efforts Explored. Edited by Henning Melber.* 2006, 56 pp, ISBN 91-7106-569-5

33. Pedro Pinto Leite, Claes Olsson, Magnus Schöldtz, Toby Shelley, Pål Wrange, Hans Corell and Karin Scheele, *The Western Sahara Conflict – The Role of Natural Resources in Decolonization. Edited by Claes Olsson.* 2006, 32 pp, ISBN 91-7106-571-7

34. Jassey, Katja and Stella Nyanzi, *How to Be a "Proper" Woman in the Times of HIV and AIDS.* 2007, 35 pp, ISBN 91-7106-574-1

35. Lee, Margaret, Henning Melber, Sanusha Naidu and Ian Taylor, *China in Africa. Compiled by Henning Melber.* 2007, 47 pp, ISBN 978-91-7106-589-6

36. Nathaniel King, *Conflict as Integration. Youth Aspiration to Personhood in the Teleology of Sierra Leone's 'Senseless War'.* 2007, 32 pp, ISBN 978-91-7106-604-6

37. Aderanti Adepoju, *Migration in sub-Saharan Africa.* 2008. 70 pp, ISBN 978-91-7106-620-6

38. Bo Malmberg, *Demography and the development potential of sub-Saharan Africa.* 2008, 39 pp, 978-91-7106-621-3

39. Johan Holmberg, *Natural resources in sub-Saharan Africa: Assets and vulnerabilities.* 2008, 52 pp, 978-91-7106-624-4

40. Arne Bigsten and Dick Durevall, *The African economy and its role in the world economy.* 2008, 66 pp, 978-91-7106-625-1

41. Fantu Cheru, *Africa's development in the 21st century: Reshaping the research agenda.* 2008, 47 pp, 978-91-7106-628-2

42. Dan Kuwali, *Persuasive Prevention. Towards a Principle for Implementing Article 4(h) and R2P by the African Union.* 2009. 70 pp. ISBN 978-91-7106-650-3

43. Daniel Volman, *China, India, Russia and the United States. The Scramble for African Oil and the Militarization of the Continent.* 2009. 24 pp. ISBN 978-91-7106-658-9

44. Mats Hårsmar, *Understanding Poverty in Africa? A Navigation through Disputed Concepts, Data and Terrains.* 2010. 54 pp. ISBN 978-91-7106-668-8

45. Sam Maghimbi, Razack B. Lokina and Mathew A. Senga, *The Agrarian Question in Tanzania? A State of the Art Paper.* 2011. 67 pp. ISBN 978-91-7106-684-8

www.ingramcontent.com/pod-product-compliance
Lightning Source LLC
Chambersburg PA
CBHW080055280326

41934CB00014B/3325